Coffee and Ink

2500 9th Avenue
Sacramento, CA 95818
(916) 452-4202

www.adavigo@earthlink.net

ISBN 0-9745722-0-9

Design and illustrations by Gail Segerstrom
Back cover photo by Jean Rosenfeld

Coffee and Ink

How a writers group

can nourish your creativity,

with tips and examples

from the

Monday Night

Writers Group

There is no pleasure in the world like writing well and going fast. It's like nothing else. It's like a love affair, it goes on and on, and doesn't end in marriage. It's all courtship.

Tennessee Williams

Contents

Introduction

Anne Da Vigo

ONE COLD MONDAY EVENING early in 1994, four writers gathered in the living room of my 1920s bungalow in midtown Sacramento, California. We drank coffee from a carafe decorated with parrots and hibiscus, stealing looks at each other as if a full-out, unthrottled meeting of the eyes would reveal too much of ourselves.

We were organizing a writers group, and this was our first meeting. We clicked our ballpoint pens and ran our thumbs over the pages of our spiral notebooks. Each of us clutched a copy of Natalie Goldberg's *Writing Down the Bones*. I imagined that sharing my writing would be like talking about my sex life in group therapy, except more embarrassing.

Eight years later, our Monday Night Writers Group still gathers from 7 to 9 p.m., pen and spiral notebook in hand. We talk writing, we critique each other's work, and always, we write. Currently, there are seven of us. Some of us are published and others not, but all of us can say it out loud, like an alcoholic admitting his addiction: we are writers.

Coffee and Ink has a two-fold purpose: to share a rich and entertaining sampling of the hundreds of pieces we have written over the years and to offer you encouragement in starting and sustaining a group of your own.

Each person in our long-ago foursome was committed to writing before we gathered that first night. Dr. Virginia Kidd was a communications studies professor at California State University and a published playwright. Adam wrote songs. Chuck was a public relations professional, and I worked as a journalist for 12 years.

We had met at an evening course, "How to Start a Writers Group," taught by Sacramento City College professor and editor-about-town Jan Haag. During the three-session course, Haag's 30 students used Natalie Goldberg's approach of writing for 20 minutes non-stop on an evocative prompt like "school lunches." It was fun. Remember the smell of overcooked fish sticks and sweaty gym socks? The taste of sour milk?

Haag kept the class safe by circulating among us to offer soothing feedback. Once the class series was over, we had a choice. Drive home and never see each other again or organize an ongoing group. Four of us agreed to meet.

The idea was attractive yet intimidating. An experienced journalist, I was confident during the 20-minute class assignments, but I was afraid that over the long term one of my really rank first drafts might slip out, larded with clichés and sagging with sentimentality. I imagined that reading my unpolished writing to a group would be like going to a party right out of bed, with my hair uncombed and mascara rings around my eyes.

And, I thought, what if some of them were better writers? Since the sixth grade, when I'd hogged the limelight in Mrs. Stock's class by reading my stories aloud, I'd shone as a writer. I won three writing awards during my newspaper career. Deep down, however, I feared I was a good craftsman but not particularly creative. I cringed at the prospect of interacting regularly with highly creative writers. I might have to face the fact that despite all my training and experience, I lacked what it took to be truly outstanding.

Besides, aren't writers supposed to struggle alone? Sit at the typewriter or computer, isolated and driven? Smoke cigarettes and grind them out in the dregs of cold coffee? Wasn't the study door supposed to be shut, closeting the writer with his angst?

What I learned, from that Monday night and about 400 Mondays since, is that a group is a writer's fat bank account, a source that we can draw on freely for support and inspiration.

Awhile back we changed the meeting night to Wednesdays for a few months to accommodate various schedules but returned to Mondays. Wednesday never felt like a writer's night to us. It lacked comfortable, worn edges like a well-thumbed page.

A few years after we started the group, members waned, so Virginia Kidd and I taught the "How to Start a Writers Group" class ourselves. From this second class we gleaned three additional members, Tom Fante, Barbara Link and Teresa Thompson, talented and committed writers who remain with us today. Later, Deb Marois and Shauna Smith became our sixth and seventh members, located through Barbara's contacts in the poetry community.

Nearly a dozen others have joined and later found the weekly commitment or the format didn't work for them, yet all have shared their talent with us and provided us with an audience and feedback for our own writing.

What we see is that the more we trust each other and ourselves, the deeper we dig into our experience and passion, the more explicit the details we put down on paper, the greater the flowering of our creativity.

From the kernels written in these twenty-minute practice sessions, we have produced poetry, short stories, essays, creative nonfiction and novels. Some have been published.

When we're discouraged, someone is there to say, "This little part is good." When we're flat and uninspired, we don't have to be brilliant; just write anything for twenty minutes. When we doubt our ability, one of our fellow writers remembers, "I'll never forget the piece you wrote about the woman in the big hat attending church and thinking about sex."

I'm not saying that a group is for everyone. But where else in life do you have your own built-in cheering section that recognizes and encourages your talent? Try it. See what happens.

Chapter 1

Operating Instructions

Anne Da Vigo

THE MONDAY NIGHT WRITERS GROUP currently arrives between 6:30 and 7 p.m. at Bella Bru, a coffee shop that sells espresso drinks, tea, and food.

We bring our notebooks and pens. Before we start, one of us may pass out a flyer for a workshop or writing contest that has appeared in our mailbox. If someone is sending out work to a contest or publisher, he may distribute a poem, chapter, or story for feedback. These we take home to read at leisure and bring back later for discussion.

Writing is the one constant when we meet. We always grab our pens for twenty minutes and write on a selected prompt. We write by the method favored by coaches like Natalie Goldberg and Anne Lamott, which encourages writing without stopping, revising, or letting our critical inner editor whisper in our ear.

We get our prompts from a collection that everyone contributes to. When the group first began, we used suggestions from Goldberg's book. Then we began collecting our own prompts and storing them in an envelope between meetings. The prompt container later became a white, cardboard takeout box stained with soy sauce. Recently, Virginia Kidd found an oval balsawood box in her closet decorated with cats, and it is now the designated prompt container.

Where do our prompt ideas come from? From *Writing Down the Bones*, and other books about writing. From sentences Barbara Link has scissored from her Christmas letters. From those thin slips of paper in fortune cookies. From calendars and snatches of conversation overheard in cafes. And from odd little thoughts that we scribble down and drop into the pile on Monday nights.

Ideally, we write twice an evening, reading what we've written to each other after each twenty-minute session.

In your own group, don't limit yourselves to writing exactly where the prompt directs you. Instead, use the prompt as a launching pad for your unconscious. You may begin writing about "My Favorite Dinner" and end up writing about your father who sliced pork roast with a bone-handled carving knife he sharpened once a week on a whetstone. Or your favorite dinner with a lover may end up as a poem about food and love. Let your pen take you where it is longing to go.

We read aloud over the chatter of the Bella Bru customers and the hiss of the espresso machine. Some nights, we are insightful and remarkably expressive. Other nights, we write the worst stuff in the Western Hemisphere, but we always keep the pen moving for twenty minutes.

In your writers group, you may get involved and not want to stop. Keep going. As the baseball players say, don't mess with a winning streak.

Some writing coaches advise listening without comment when group members read. Others suggest critiques, both good and bad. Our practice has evolved over many years to commenting on the parts that particularly impressed or touched us or tickled our funny bone.

We save our negative criticism, along with positive commentary, for material that members have been writing at home with revisions and bring to the group with a request for feedback. (More on feedback later.)

Our group has found that Monday night meetings have also evolved into a round table where we share tips from other authors, recommendations on new books or movies and examples of good (or bad) writing we have encountered in the past week.

As you become acquainted with your own group, you will discover you have a cheering section to celebrate your successes, large and small. You may notice, as you continue to write, that your family and friends, while they wish you the best, don't always understand your commitment to writing or why an editor's encouraging sentence in a rejection notice is a cause for hope rather than despair.

No matter what else you do with your group, always write together and read aloud what you've written. Writing focuses you on your purpose. It keeps your group from letting its writing muscle degenerate and ending up as a chat group, a therapy session, or a dialog about why you can't get any writing done.

Twenty minutes. Twice. You've done it!

Chapter 2

Getting Started

Using a Writing Prompt to Start a Twenty-Minute Writing Practice

Anne Da Vigo

WHEN ONE OF US dips his fingers into the prompt box and pulls out a slip of folded paper, we never know what to expect. Anyone in the group is welcome to contribute prompts and they have different flavors, like dishes at a potluck.

We may find a good idea in one of Natalie Goldberg or Julia Cameron's books. Deb may contribute a philosophical saying. Teresa has a metaphysical bent and her contributions to the prompt box reflect this.

Virginia, a communications professor, has come up with some novel ways to generate writing topics, including bringing a handful of fortune cookies. Each of us broke the cookie and wrote on his fortune. Another evening she toted along small plastic bags containing various herbs and spices.

Some Monday nights the prompt is read and everyone groans. Despite drawing an apparently difficult topic, we rarely pass, because the most obscure prompt may generate the most interesting writing.

In your group, look at the prompt as a starting point, not a strait jacket. You may begin with a prompt, "Describe a Childhood Friend," and discover what you really want to write about is a person who has been betrayed by a close friend.

On any one prompt, you may choose to write a poem, a list, a dialog, or a description. The words flowing from your pen may take shape as an essay, character sketch, or the seed of a short story or novel. Your piece could be from your personal viewpoint or the viewpoint of a fictional character. It can be anything you want. Just keep writing for twenty minutes.

For a list of some of our favorite prompts, turn to page 91.

Chapter 3

Murder, Mystery and Marriage

Five Examples of Writing to a Prompt

Anne Da Vigo

MARK TWAIN AND HIS BUDDY, William Dean Howells, had a great idea for a competition among their writer pals. They'd get a "good and godly gang" of them together and they'd each write a story on a pre-determined topic. The stories were to be published in an 1876 edition of *The Atlantic Monthly*.

Twain's topic: A Murder, a Mystery, and a Marriage.

He grabbed his quill pen and wrote to Oliver Wendell Holmes, James Russell Lowell (what is it with the three names?), Bret Harte, and Henry James, but couldn't capture their interest.

So he wrote the novella himself, but it apparently was never published. The manuscript, through a series of mishaps, was separated into two parts, one of which lay in a trunk gathering dust in a Buffalo, New York attic for a hundred years or so. Someone found the missing half, united the manuscript and *The Atlantic Monthly* published the work in 2001.

Here's what the good and godly gang from the Monday Night Writers Group produced using Twain's long-ago prompt, which in our version is the more global "Murder, Mystery, and Marriage." (Note: some of these have been polished slightly and others are pretty much the way they came from the pen, minus the misspellings and plus a few commas.)

Murder, Mystery, and Marriage

Viginia Kidd

*I*f it weren't for a convenient murder, I would still be married to Donny Bryer, known to some as the Don of the Briar Patch. Since I walked away clear with a quarter mil of the green and free of his lying ass, I'm not too keen on tracking down his killer. Oh, I have to put on a front for Sheriff McGonikal's sake, not too heavy, they all know Don had been cheating on me since he made it with the stripper who popped out of his bachelor cake, and they know I know about some of them, but hey, if Hillary could look right into the camera and smile, I can look into it and force out a tear or two.

I figure it was a friend who did him in. A friend of mine, I mean. Donny dropped me off that night at my Tai Chi class, which everybody, including Nita "Big Mouth" Bass, saw plainly. He was dead before I finished my after-workout cranberry-yogurt smoothie, so I was one of the few people—along with the rest of the Tai Chi class—who had no opportunity to end Donny's infidelity for good.

So now I'm rich, and free, and unencumbered, and somebody else took all the risks. I'd like to know who it was. I'd like to thank that friend who met Donny down by Clauson Creek, leaned over the side of the '96 Pontiac Firebird, and put a bullet right straight into that cavity where Donny should have had a heart.

Murder, Mystery, and Marriage

Barbara Link

*T*he wild ponies galloped through the wavering fog. Short, stocky horses, their huge heads bobbed like the shaggy, gray waves on our North Carolina beach.

Riley grabbed my hand and pointed to the lead pony, "See, there she is, the little girl." I held up my thumb and forefinger in front of my right eye. The quarter- inch aperture helped my near- sighted vision. He was right. Her wet yellow hair plastered her high forehead and matched the yellow rain coat that billowed out behind her little shape.

I turned away jerking Riley's warm, brown hand behind me. "No," I said, "there's no little girl, Riley, no little girl."

"But...but, I saw her. She's riding Cheerio."

"Riley, there was a little girl but she's gone. Her family moved to Charleston after—after she left."

"Can I ride Cheerio?"

"Maybe later. When he comes up to the porch for carrots, I'll help you catch him. But now, I need your help to pick up shells. We need lots of crunchy shells to scatter for Sissie when she walks down the aisle tomorrow with Landon."

☙

Murder, Mystery, and Marriage

Anne Da Vigo

*S*unny tripped over her ex-husband and fell on the bedroom rug. At least, she assumed it was Leon, because the body was naked and not that many men showed up that way in her bedroom – only one, in fact. She crawled closer. Ouch, she'd scraped her knee. Her eyes strained in the dim illumination from the street light.

Leon lay on his stomach, his beefy arms at his sides and his size 13 feet pointing in like a child snoozing in its crib. It was hard to imagine Leon as a child.

She'd met him at a bluegrass festival near Angel's Camp while she was lying on her grandmother's patchwork quilt spread on meadow grass that was browning in the summer heat. He stretched out nearby, propped on one elbow, his dusty black boots crossed in front of him. A flat bottle of Jack Daniels protruded from the pocket of his leather vest.

A biker. Sunny had shivered with fascinated repulsion. A tuft of straight, dark hair curled from under his armpit. They had danced, sung along with the bands and drunk JD until 2 a.m.

One of her calves touched his thigh. Her mind did a strange little sum, adding up the details. She sprawled on the wall-to-wall Berber with the man she had once loved. A breath of light from the streetlight out front reflected off his balding head and his silver ponytail. Silver?

Sunny giggled, her sides shaking and her feet tapping against Leon's thigh and she couldn't stifle her laughter and after awhile tears ran into her mouth and she couldn't tell if she were laughing or crying.

She had no doubt he was dead. There was a stillness about him, as if his molecules had stopped their movement, and Leon had never been still. During dinner he'd jump up from the table, a chicken leg in one hand, and make telephone calls. He clicked the television remote control constantly, so quickly Sunny gave up trying to make sense of any of the shows. Instead, she pretended she was watching a strange, surreal MTV video. Leon never came to bed before three, and when he slept, his fingers and feet twitched.

Why wasn't she surprised he was here? She hadn't seen him in five years, since he'd turned over the house keys in the hall outside divorce court. She remembered the keys in her palm, still warm from the pocket of his black leather pants.

But she'd heard about him. The creepy DEA agent with bitten nails and starched white shirt told her Leon was living in the Sierra near Wilseyville. The feds were looking for a million-dollar suitcase of cash Leon had supposedly brought from Canada.

He'd always had secrets. His motorcycle repair place in a Rancho Cordova industrial park that the police said was a chop shop. The younger brother he'd never told her about who died during their teen years while they were racing bikes on a mountain road.

He'd hidden things in the house, too. One rainy January night after their separation, Leon knocked on the kitchen door, wet hair plastered to his head. He said he wanted to have a Bud for old times' sake. When he took his jacket off, he smelled of strange chemicals. He climbed the stairs to use the bathroom, and when he came down, Sunny had ignored a bulge that appeared under his shirt.

Somewhere in the neighborhood, a dog barked, short, irregular sounds, as if the animal was looking for a reason to make noise. Sunny thought about turning Leon over, but couldn't gather the strength. There might be a wound or blood. She didn't want to know.

∽

Murder, Mystery, and Marriage

Deb Marois

*I*t's a mystery to me. How is it that two people can be so in love and then, in just a few short years, they end up separated, practically hating each other despite not really knowing the other at all?" Julie's brown eyes darkened, and in them I could see the sadness, liquidy pools of heartache pleading for an answer.

Unfortunately, I wasn't sure she was ready to hear my opinions. After all, is there anything more mysterious than a marriage? It is a wonder that any couple manages to stay together for any length of time. I certainly can't imagine fifty-six years—the longest marriage I'd heard of in recent memory. All that time for the little resentments to pile up, a garbage heap covered by a tent-sized tarp (never mind sweeping under the rug, it's gone way beyond that). Each passing day, small niceties die and are buried under a mushrooming mound of bitterness. These days, it seems like "healthy marriage" is nearly an oxymoron, like "male intellect."

"Jules, you can't possibly try to figure it out anymore. You have all the answers you're ever going to have. Just put it behind you now and move on." I said it firmly, but not without compassion. She needed to hear this. I watched her chin quiver. Suddenly, Jules burst into a torrent of tears, sobs that had lurked barely below the surface, stored up and just waiting for the moment to escape. "It hurts so much." She drew in a deep breath, "I want to hurt him as much as he's hurt me." Jules looked away, avoiding my gaze. "There are times when reason leaves me. Instead I hear a cold voice that freezes my heart. Sometimes, I think about his dying." She wasn't crying any more. "I stay up at night, fantasizing," she confessed haltingly, "imagining all the ways I could make him suffer."

"Jules! Can you hear yourself? Don't you know that you don't need him? He's just bringing you down, girl. Can't you see that?" I wasn't smiling any more and the urgency in my voice forced her to look at me. "This is not healthy for you, and you need to take care of yourself. Once you put him out of your life and out of your heart for good, you can concentrate on finding a lasting relationship."

I doubted my words could penetrate the cloak of grief that was wrapped so tightly around Jules. Besides, "lasting relationship" might be another oxymoron. How could I convince her to have hope? If by some miracle, a marriage does endure then perhaps what you have is a compost heap instead

of a garbage pile. And instead of covering it up, you get out in it and stomp
around in it once in a while. You don't let it pile up too much, and you use it
to live in each other's lives. You're careful about what you put in there.
Certain things are not appropriate for the compost pile; those things get
thrown out all together.

I watched silently as a new flood of tears flowed freely down her cheeks.

∽◉

Murder, Mystery, and Marriage

Tom Fante

The whole thing started when my girlfriend's head floated to the surface of Boggy Slough. It was late January and she'd been missing a couple of weeks. She'd gone for a walk "to take in the waters," she said. She got more than she bargained for. She had wanted to think about what she called my "non-offer" of marriage. I didn't want to marry her, of course. "What's to marry?" I asked. "I'm rich; you're young and hot," (so I supposed), but what she replied gave me pause (as a man, I paused).

"I'm older than I look," she said.

"How much older?" I asked. Then I squinted—there were telltale wrinkles and hairline cracks that radiated from her yellow-hued eyes. It was curious that I'd never noticed them before, but maybe that was because she had such a perfect figure. Suddenly, I saw that those irises I thought blue were, was it brown? Green? And they were swimming in that yellow-colored eyeball. (So I got her point and that's why I paused.)

Was she too old for me? (In years, she was twenty years younger, but all those little wrinkles and that yellow hue concerned me. Yes, they gave me doubts. I wondered if I'd made a mistake.) Such was what I was feeling on the day she disappeared. She had gone without leaving a trace. She'd become a "missing person" and (potentially) the object of foul play. (Or so the rumors in the press suggested.)

It was only too obvious that her power increased the further away (I almost said "the deader") she seemed. Gone and possibly dead, she took on a life of her own, so to speak, and grew more and more menacing. She was going to be the death of me! Didn't she know that marriage was out of the question? I was already married, for God's sake! (The marriage wasn't my idea.) But in the eyes of the voters, the sovereign people (for whom its voice is the voice of God!), I was married, sentenced, condemned, chained to an old and perpetually menopausal crone.

I needed a young thing, but you don't look for sympathy from the "great unwashed" as they are so aptly called. Did I kill her? Not according to the lie detector test my lawyer gave me. I was proved innocent! And by now, if she were drowned, she was in too deep, deep down, under the waves, a feast for worms, fresh-water snails, fish, and diving turtles, but, like a bad penny, her head turned up one day in the slough, and how does one go about explaining that? She wasn't wearing cement booties or a lead kimono, but the missing half of her seemed to imply something heavy.

Suspicion came my way. I knew it would, but though it wouldn't be easy, I resolved for the sake of my children to tough it out and deny everything. As for the scandal, there was nothing I could do about that.

So I said, "She was such a lovely girl," and offered a big reward for the capture of her killer. I owed her that much. It was going to be a long winter. I was sure of that, but if winter comes, can spring be far behind?

☙

Chapter 4

The Good Stuff: Benefits of a Writers Group

Anne Da Vigo

MY HUSBAND, Tony, usually is sitting at the kitchen table on Mondays when I gather up my spiral notebook, my ballpoint pen, and my purse. I've made a quick dinner of spaghetti topped with Prego tomato and mushroom sauce, and I'm off to writers group.

"So," he says, "are you going to learn how to write tonight?" He is kidding, but he also has a quizzical look on his face. I think it means, what could you possibly have to say or do with a bunch of other scribblers after eight years of Monday nights?

One evening, the group answered that question when we decided to write for twenty minutes on "The Benefits of a Writers Group." As you will see when you read this set of pieces, each of us draws a different kind of inspiration and nourishment from our Monday nights. Read them with your own needs in mind. What part of your writing life is the most difficult? You will find that your own vulnerable writer's spot—the one that brings up all the fear and self-loathing about what a rotten writer you are—is the one that will slowly unwind and smooth out when you write with others.

Benefits of a Writers Group

Anne Da Vigo

There are days, sometimes weeks, when I can barely put my fingers on the computer keys. I look at my desk, a cheap, composition number that my daughter left behind, and I hate every inch of it. Especially the little glob of glue that escaped when we assembled the drawer.

If I do manage to press the computer's power switch and get into Microsoft Word, every sentence seems as heavy as a hunk of stone. My menopausal hot flashes start, and I'm convinced I'll never write another good sentence. That's when the writers group comes to my rescue.

"Remember that wonderful piece you wrote about Thanksgiving dinner?" Virginia says one night at writers group. I think, she's right. That piece wasn't half bad.

Encouragement and common experience are two of the benefits of writing together and sharing our successes. And failures. Tom is the group's Attila the Hun editor. I usually get a glass of chardonnay before I read his critiques because he goes over our work with a ruthless pen. Almost always, however, he has caught a misplaced detail, an unclear reference, or a factual error. My work is always better for his scrutiny.

Barb helps me get in touch with the crazy, weird, funny part of myself that creates writing that is fun to read.

Deb and Teresa have a calm, thoughtful viewpoint that encourages me to dig deeper, stir up a few more ant's nests from my past. The writers group calls me to write more truly, more deeply, and with less gimmickry.

∞

Benefits of a Writers Group

Barbara Link

*S*oy, hoison, or black bean sauce? Our Chinese take-out box of writing prompts has a brown stain in the corner. Whatever the stain is, the effect of those prompts from the box is many, many twenty-minute masterpieces our writing group has composed since its conception about eight years ago.

Yes, can you believe it? We meet every week, every Monday in a cafe that serves roast beef sandwiches, Russian tea cakes, and dinosaur cookies. We listen to the espresso machine gurgle and hiss and complain about the cold, noise and vegetarian chili. Last week I had the vegetable quiche served on three pieces of wilted red lettuce.

After the food, the general discussion: How was your family holiday? Did you have a Christmas fight? (My answer was YES!) Then we remove a prompt from the stained box and begin. Any writing is allowed—you can follow the suggested prompt or not. For myself, I vowed never to refuse a prompt. I can never say it's too hard or I can't think of anything to write, or it won't be good anyway. Usually I just start and see where the writing takes me. For the past five years, I've accumulated little snippets that I've incorporated into my poems, my novel-in-progress, my completed non-fiction book and my collection of short stories.

Now I can legitimately say I'm a writer when asked about my profession. I always knew I was, but it was a secret to the world. WRITER, I say. I write, I'm published, and I'm a member of a WRITING GROUP.

☙

Benefits of a Writers Group

Virginia Kidd

The siren wailed past on G Street, loud enough to invade closed windows and circle the silent living room. I sat against the arm of the blue couch writing on a stiff-backed pad, encouraged by Cassius, the long-haired apricot cat who momentarily blessed me with his chin on my thigh. I don't remember now what I wrote, but I remember in detail what I learned when the group members each began to read our work: the siren had screamed its way into Chuck's piece—the siren, the rumbling train down by 20th, the sharp click of Cassius' nails when he leapt to the hardwood floor. The world Anne created was fragrant, redolent of fresh gardenias and roses, the cinnamon and lavender of melting candles, the aromas of hot baking bread, garlic, and oregano. In contrast, in my writing, characters subsisted on Coca-cola and chocolate in a world virtually environment-free and soundless except for dialogue. In the writing group, I learned to let my characters hear chairs creak and leaves rattle, smell cat litter and fresh strawberries, feel heat and cold and rain and snow, taste angel food cake and rutabaga, run their fingers over rugged bark and the smooth glass of a mirror.

Sometimes I wrote of my life as a child, and having to set the story somewhere, I chose Baytown, Texas, that ordinary, dull place where I grew up; to the group, however, Baytown was not ordinary and not dull. A town dominated by Humble Oil, where most fathers refined gasoline, where humidity was as thick as southern drawls, and the high school was named for Robert E. Lee, seemed fascinating to people born in Colorado and upstate New York and California, and even to Army brats who had roamed the streets of Memphis and Germany. I learned I have stories to tell that are not as ordinary as I thought.

I have learned to appreciate a wider variety of writing forms—nature descriptions, poetry, list poems, personal essays based on family or childhood or work, short stories, even romance.

Most of all, I get from the group, briefly, a respite from my own hypocrisy of pretending an interest in conversations about curtains, or diets or a wonderful snorkeling adventure in Honolulu. In the group I can give voice to the subject that haunts my consciousness: the intricacies of how words work together on paper. I can discuss with people who understand and care about the challenge and power of writing. In a world where success is measured by financial achievement, I get confirmation for struggling with words to create the magic of writing.

☙

Benefits of a Writers Group

Tom Fante

1. Hundreds of little "seed" stories, some combined and some developed into longer ones.

2. A better sense of how the creative process can be pushed into happening.

3. Sometimes it is the hardest or the dullest piece that has the greatest potential for further development.

4. Sometimes a little story has an ending; sometimes not. It is the stories that don't end that have the greatest potential.

5. The assistance and support of a group of like-minded people are important over the long haul.

6. A sense of what to write about, what sorts of things come out, if allowed to do so.

7. It is hard to write outside my habitual boundaries.

8. Writing on despite the noise of other peoples' conversations and the clank of plates and cups, knives and forks, the roar of the espresso machine, and unpleasant loud music.

9. It is important to write regularly, even if infrequently, so that the practice doesn't disappear entirely.

10. Be a better listener by recognizing how bad a listener you are.

11. You never know where you're going when you start or where you'll end a story till you get there.

12. Writing is created to be edited or tossed away.

13. Most everything I write is bad in some way.

14. A good idea is not a good story.

15. If you are hand writing something, it is a good idea to write slowly and clearly, so you can read it later.

Benefits of a Writers Group

Deb Marois

A few years ago, as a recent transplant to Sacramento, I found my way to the Monday Night Writers Group. As the newest and also youngest member, I reap the benefit of everyone's experience and longevity not only in writing, but also in life. The group makes me realize I have a long way to go.

The primary benefit to me is the continual encouragement to keep writing, try new techniques, and expand my horizons as a writer. Since my solitary writing practice usually centers on journaling, it's a welcome stretch to explore dialogue, focus on detail, and write from different points of view.

Meeting weekly has helped me reclaim—at least a little—the self-image of "writer." Amid the whir of espresso machines and the buzz arising from dozens of simultaneous conversations, my voice reads aloud my captured thoughts that are usually written for my eyes only. The group's feedback helps to nurture this budding identity no matter how slow the pace.

The members are also a rich source of knowledge about area bookstores, current films, writing workshops, local history, and state politics, among other topics. As a newcomer to Sacramento, getting involved with a writing group was a great way to meet people I'd never know otherwise, push my self-imposed boundaries as a writer, and make new friends in the process.

Best of all, writing nights serve as a type of stress relief. For a few hours each week, I don't have to think about work, relationships, or household chores. I only have to put pen to paper and let everything else go.

Benefits of a Writers Group

Teresa Thompson

I write, and when I write, my world grows larger, and I expand too. I write like I dance—freely, openly, with big leaps and turns. I can turn a phrase, write a line to start a poem, or even write a whole poem. I glide around words, watch them drip from my tongue, and touch the ground. I twirl and float and move words around to the beginning or the end of a sentence. Or I break the words apart and make my own words, create my own world.

In this world of words, nothing is perfect or pure. Anything can be changed. I can be black, white, or in-between. I can be a man or a woman. These possibilities feed me. The ideas for writing make me a better person, one who looks for details, but also looks behind the details to search for broader meaning, for the mystery of small things.

∞

Writing Examples

Anne DaVigo

MY HOUSE IS FILLED with unfinished projects. Ten years ago I started a quilt. Six of the nine squares are done; the rest are in scraps and bits. In my study sits a large box of dried hydrangea blossoms I was going to use in two dried arrangements, but I never completed them.

I've written parts of two novels that are sitting in my computer waiting for me to pay them some attention. I've got a shelf of notebooks full of twenty-minute writings that have the embryo of a good story if I ever took the time to develop them.

The fact is, finishing things is scary. There are wonderful phrases that don't fit once the story unfolds. They have to be cut, and you're sure you'll never write anything as insightful again. A character is superfluous and taking him out is like losing a friend. But most of all, you're afraid your finished piece won't be as good as you had hoped.

You want it to funny, and you're afraid it will fall flat. You want your heroine to be flesh and bone and contradictions, but as you put your fingers on the keyboard, she's a paper doll.

Your writers group can help you here. Let the members know what you're up to and ask them for some supportive nagging. Often, they will remember your piece and be curious to see how you develop it.

Once you've started, bring a draft for them to read. A committed reader can give you a creative lift, because they have a glimpse of your vision. You can accept or reject their comments, but either way, your idea becomes clearer, like a landscape as the sun comes up.

This section features pieces that began as a twenty-minute writing session. The writers leafed through their notebooks, picked one they particularly liked and finished it.

She Wished He Was Back

(Prompt: In a State of Disarray)

Teresa Thompson

She wished he was back
His voice played in her head
like a sax played sideways,
Husky and rough,
calling her

They drank cold ones in a
Small dark bar and he laughed
as he smoked

his eyes squinting against
the flame of the lighter
His lips big and black and
luscious

As she inhaled his scent
His clean dark skin seemed to
shine in the evening light

As she inhaled his scent
his clean
dark
skin
seemed to shine

∽

Biding Time

(Prompt: It Was the Best Time of Day, It Was the Worst Time of Day)

Deb Marois

*F*umbling with the keys, she juggles her various packages and tries to unlock the door. Filtered sunlight briefly warms the back of her neck. The door slowly swings open, and the bags tumble inside. She impatiently brushes the waiting cats aside so she can enter her sanctuary.

It's the end of the work day, and evening holds great promise. Briefly scanning her mail, she runs upstairs to check her phone messages and e-mail. Communication from the outside world is often mildly disappointing, but that never dampens her hopes for more.

The computer beckons. No matter that she has spent the better part of the day in front of a glowing screen. Now, she is unconstrained by the demands of work. She can investigate the universe from her makeshift office. Instead, she flips on some music and pulls up a game of solitaire. Sipping a beer and occasionally indulging in a forbidden cigarette, she loses herself in the hypnotic challenge of cards flying across the screen. Like the constant flow of a river making its way to the ocean, her mind wanders and empties.

Time passes, first one hour, then two. Hunger sets in and she realizes the early evening is gone. Soon, it's late and she hasn't gone for that bike ride, cooked dinner, or paid much attention to the cats. She hasn't read something enlightening, done research, meditated, or sketched. But she has grasped something she has difficultly defining: blessed alone time, relieved of the necessity to work, with no one to answer to and no responsibilities. She achieves a state of numbness.

For now, this is how she treats her grief.

∐

Bringing Home the Fiancé

(Prompt: Bringing Home the Fiancé)

Barbara Link

*S*ean and Carla waved little flags at each other from opposite ends of the mall. They always met after their college classes where both had undeclared majors. The flag system was to help enter each other's aura. Carla's flag was mauve, meaning she was feeling extra detached today. Sean's flag was an anxious orange.

"You're perfect!" Sean said when they eventually met. "Your baby blue twin set shows off the pearls and those boobs! Can I touch them?" he pleaded.

"Not right now. Not in the food court," Carla said. She stepped back and stroked her upper arm. "All my sweaters are cashmere."

Sean smoothed the air over Carla's arm. "Today's the day we go to meet them, my parents."

Carla swirled her french fry in mayo. "I'm only doing it because Cosmo says that's the next step in a real relationship."

"My mom will stare at your pearls. Don't be surprised if she grabs a strand and rubs it on her teeth."

"Jesus God, is she a homo? She'd better not touch me!"

"Women aren't homo. They're dykes. Dad'll stare at your chest. He'll hug you to see if they're real." Sean stacked ketchup packages. He had five in a tower before it fell.

"You know how I hate to be fondled. Remember that little Japanese boy on the plane? He kept trying to rub my ear lobe!" Carla shuddered. "I wish I had a plastic bubble to slip over me when I'm in public.

"So, what are they like?" Carla petted her other cashmere arm. "They're not Lutherans, are they?"

Sean jammed his hands into his pockets and stared into the fish tank. They'd finished lunch and were standing in front of the pet store. His eyes darted after the angel fish. "Oh, I don't know. Just parents, you'll see."

The door was red. Good feng shui. No one answered their knock.

"Oh, that's right!" Sean fingered his earring. "They faxed me about that. They don't use doors anymore."

He pulled her around to the side yard and boosted her up through an open window. She fell into a dark room with black felt-lined walls that smelled like the inside of a dirty refrigerator; she was eye to eye with a stuffed baby seal. Sean thumped beside her, then carefully righted the small replica of an Eskimo he had knocked over.

"This is the Admiral Byrd Alter Ego Exhibit. It used to be my room."

"Holy Mother Macree! I'm not up for this right now. I'm pre-menstrual." She pulled the soft cashmere over her ribs. Her waist was as small as Scarlet O'Hara's. "And I'm post-coital."

"Okay, we'll go the shortcut. But we have to crawl. Crawl carefully through the Amazon Basin that used to be the front hall and watch for pygmies."

"Sean? I'm—I'm not—." She scooted after the disappearing bottoms of his tennis shoes. The right one was patched with duct tape.

"Ouch!" Carla grabbed at her neck.

"You're hit." Sean turned around and examined the tiny feather dart. "You know, your neck is as long and white as Audrey Hepburn's." He removed the dart. " Now we cross the river. Follow me."

They snaked low in the dark until the floor gave way. They slid down a metal chute and hit water.

Carla surfaced with her tented hands. Her Ketchup in the Snow polish glistened twelve days after her last manicure.

"I'm melting, Sean." She spit water and dog paddled. "My outfit!"

"I know, I know, I know. I'll buy you another one. Swim to the bank. Watch for coelacanths."

Carla side-stroked thick, green water like a swimming student. She had turning and breathing down perfectly when her hand touched the side. Sean was already beached. He yanked his fiancée out on a bank covered with green indoor-outdoor carpet and plastic ferns.

Carla's hair streamed like wet shoelaces. "You're lucky my eyeliner is tattooed, otherwise I'd have raccoon eyes."

The Lindstroms paddled up in their canoe and stared at Carla like she was the bride of Neptune.

"Nice pearls," Mrs. Lindstrom said.

"Nice tits," Mr. Lindstrom said.

They liked her.

The Gumshoe and the Bookdrop

(Prompt: Someone's Routine is Interrupted and his or her Life is Changed Forever)

Virginia Kidd

Mrs. Edna Pierce carefully squeezed past the juvenile non-fiction shelves and turned at the door into the kitchen. She still thought of it as the kitchen, although the library director, Ona Wiggins, called it the workroom. Really! It had the white tile counters with black trim put in when the mansion was built and a big wide sink below a window that looked out onto cobalt blue morning glories. And, of course, a computer station and a desk, and a wooden work table. But still—.

She took the bookdrop key off the brass hook, holding it by the gray plastic identifying tag. The bookdrop, with its weekend cache of books and the Sunday newspaper, was always first on her agenda. She stepped out the back door, strolled past the French doors that opened to the children's collection, turned onto the brick patio by the alley, and stopped abruptly.

The bookdrop was gone!

The possibility was so foreign to Mrs. Pierce's mind that she simply stared, dangling the key at her side. Finally she walked to the alley and looked both ways. No bookdrop.

This was simply not possible. The bookdrop was bigger than a postal box, screwed into concrete, and generally, after the weekend, filled to overflowing with books. It would be very, very heavy.

She walked to the street and peered left and right. Oh dear. Oh dear, this was going to be very bad, very bad. Ona Wiggins would simply shit.

What had she said? She had to stop reading private-eye novels. Her internal language was deteriorating beyond acceptability.

Well, Ona shouldn't be such an uptight bitch. No, no that's not what she meant.

Determinedly she marched through the fresh morning air back into the library. She punched in 9-1-1.

The answering voice had a sharp edge. "Police. Is this an emergency?"

"Certainly," Edna Pierce replied with equal sharpness. "Otherwise I would have dialed 264-7219." The numbers stared at her from the bulletin board. Strictly speaking, this was not an emergency like a car accident or a bank robbery where time was critical, but declaring it an emergency was undoubtedly the only way to get the attention of those donut-licking assholes. Stop it!

"What is the trouble, ma'am?" The voice was female, impatient.

'The Oakville Library bookdrop has been stolen."

Just as she feared, this was met with silence. "I'm sorry. Could you repeat?"

"The bookdrop has been stolen! Before it was even emptied!"

"But—who would—how could—who would steal a bookdrop?"

"Exactly!" The girl had a modicum of sense although she seemed very slow on the uptake.

"Well, I'm not at all sure what we can do."

"I suspect,"—Mrs. Pierce's voice was firm, her pronunciation crisp—"that it contained drugs." She didn't really approve of lying, but it was clear she had to prod these friggin' shitheads. Oh! No more hard-boiled detectives. None!

"I'll see if someone is free to stop by."

The voice still did not recognize the urgency of this situation. Mrs. Pierce would have to speak harshly. "Get off your fucking ass, Barbie-brain, and get some of those dickhead cops down here NOW!"

She sank against the wall. How could she have said that aloud? Stiffly, the dispatch operator requested her name.

In her most clear diction, Mrs. Pierce replied, "Ona Wiggins," gave her boss's phone number and hung up.

Ona would be furious when she found out, but really, Edna Pierce could not stay around all day getting the third degree from the fuzz. Down those mean streets she must go, to snag herself a .44 Magnum. She had a library to protect.

⊘

Delia

(Prompt: Change a Character by Changing his or her Name)

Anne Da Vigo

*D*elia sat by the kitchen fireplace and stirred the embers. Silence settled around her like a soft cloak. A few minutes earlier, her stepsisters, Eunice and Harriet, had clattered out the front door, their high-heeled shoes clacking on the stone floors like horses' hooves on the street.

All day, the house had been bursting with sound. Harriet screeched at the dressmaker over the flounces and ruching on her ballgown. Eunice wailed for hours, claiming the hairdresser had ruined her wig. Delia's stepmother appeared at the top of the servants' staircase every few minutes to bellow instructions: "Delia! Where are you, you stupid girl? Hurry up with those milk baths," and, "You fool! The complexion poultice is too hot! Harriet's skin is ruined."

Weeks ago, the king's white-gloved messengers had knocked on the doors of all eligible young women in the kingdom. They delivered gold-engraved invitations to tonight's ball at the royal palace. Delia's stepmother and stepsisters had whirled in a state of frenzy ever since. Word was that the King and Queen had given the Crown Prince an ultimatum–give up his carefree life composing songs and playing the flute and take a bride. This was the opportunity Harriet and Eunice had been waiting for.

To snare him for one of her daughters, Delia's stepmother spent every spare guilder, even the dowry Delia's father had set aside for her before he died. Shoemakers and dressmakers jostled each other on the stairs. Jewelers and glovemakers hauled their sample cases in and out of the sitting room. The moneylender had slipped quietly through the kitchens and up to her stepmother's quarters, wrapped in a long, dark cloak.

Delia sighed and loosened the long braid that hung down her back. Her hair glittered like gold in the low light as she combed her fingers through the strands. The touch of her hair on her neck reminded her of long ago when she had sat on a silk cushion in front of the fire in her ivory and Dresden bedroom while the maid had combed her hair with a tortoise shell comb. Now, Delia regretted that she had snapped at the girl when the comb's teeth caught in a snarl and pulled her scalp.

Delia rose from her wooden stool and shook out her faded blue homespun dress. Soft from much washing, it clung to her thighs. At the long worktable, she began peeling apples. They were the best of the crop, picked at dawn with her own hands. Ruby curls of skin fell away from her flashing knife blade. The fruit's perfume rose around her and the juices dripped on the scarred tabletop. She cored the apples with quick motions and cut them into thin slices.

Next, she carried chunks of split wood to the fireplace and, blowing gently, coaxed the fire to a snapping blaze. Soon the kitchen was filled with a nimbus of light. Dancing shadows flickered over the iron pots, the baskets of dried nuts and fruits, and the bunched herbs hanging from the rafters.

Delia sifted flour to remove any stray chaff, added a pinch of salt, and worked in some sweet butter. Her fingers squeezed and pressed the dough in a soothing rhythm until it formed a smooth ball.

She spread her fingers for a moment to look at her hands. They were lean, and the backs were dotted with freckles from the sun. When her father was alive, they were white and plump, covered with kid gloves if she had ventured outside.

She assembled the pie, pinching the crust into a fluted rim and lacing pastry crosswise over the top. The long-handled paddle scraped on the brick as the pie slid into the oven beside the fireplace. Soon its scent crept through the air.

Delia used a ladle to dip a basin of hot water from a cauldron over the fire. As she rolled up her sleeves and unbuttoned the collar of her dress, the cool air touched her skin. With a piece of linen salvaged from an old tablecloth, she washed her arms and then her face, letting her skin freshen in the steam. She took a wooden comb from the small cupboard that contained her only belongings. Her hair threw off little sparks as she drew the comb through it. She tied it back with a scrap of blue satin ribbon discarded from Eunice's ballgown.

She should be sorrier. Her goose-down bed, the richly-sauced dinners, the rows of pastel gowns to complement her delicate complexion, all were gone. She had never known her mother, who died in childbirth. Her father, she remembered in faint glimpses, his face through a half-open door as he talked to men with jeweled rings on their fingers or his figure towering over her as she curtsied.

What she recalled most vividly about her old life was the boredom. Mornings, she had learned insipid tunes on the clavichord or received instruction in etiquette. During the afternoon she practiced her embroidery. A maid had followed her everywhere and scolded her if she ran and jumped to stretch her strong young legs or leaned out the casement window to allow the sun to tickle her eyelids.

Delia's life now was sometimes bleak, but it also contained moments of magic. This morning the orchard had been hushed, clad in a low-lying autumn mist. As she plucked apples from the branches, the damp yellow-green leaves had brushed her face, as gentle as a fairy's touch.

Early in the summer she had been returning from the fish market when the sound of a flute tumbled over the wall of the king's castle. The tune was a merry melody that made Delia snap her fingers and tap her toes. She put the wrapped fish on the cobblestones, kicked off her heavy clogs, and began to dance. She whirled and dipped, her braid bouncing against her back, her feet flying in an intricate pattern that seemed to have been born in her bones. She felt as free as the swallows that soared over the town in wide, swooping arcs.

The last of the flute's notes hovered in the air. She looked up and saw a young man with rumpled brown hair peering over the parapet at her. From where she stood on the dusty road, he appeared to be richly dressed in a hunter green tunic.

A log thumped in the fireplace. Delia remembered her pie and peered in the oven. Juices were bubbling through the lattice crust. A few more minutes. Suddenly, there was a knock at the kitchen door. She lifted the iron bar and pulled it open. The hinges creaked. A rush of cold air rippled the folds of her skirt.

"Welcome, your highness," she said, and closed the door quietly behind the Crown Prince.

∽

Living Off Center

(Prompt: A Brief Encounter)

Shauna L. Smith

It is close to midnight and my husband and I are exhausted and frustrated after several hours of primitive efforts at trying to throw clay. We still can't tell if the clay is too wet or too dry, too thin or too thick, how fast or slow to run the wheel, how to open and close the clay correctly or how to center. I for one am convinced that if someone will just teach us to center properly, everything else will follow.

Greg, another resident at the Mendocino Art Center, is still at work on his pottery and I ask if he would give us a lesson on the wheel the next day. While he is mulling this over, a small, powerful-looking man in his mid-thirties walks through the door. "Hey there, Masaki," Greg calls out enthusiastically, and then, inspired, turns back to us. "Here before us is the Master. Ask him to give you a lesson. That's the way to really learn."

We look respectfully at the beautiful strong man who sizes us up as he passes by to check on his work. We find that the huge bowls we have been admiring, which are cut through into forms that seem to mirror our unconscious universe, are his. We have just met the Japanese Master everyone has been talking about; the sculptor who has been traveling around the world lecturing, teaching, and demonstrating.

We are about to leave the clay room when Masaki appears at our side. "So, you want to learn?" he addresses me.

"Yes," I assure him. "Yes, we do."

"Okay. Where's your clay?"

"Now?" I glance at the clock—12:10 a.m.

"You want to learn, right? What do you have for the wheel?"

I watch my hand point to the left. Masaki walks over and looks through several bags of leftover clay stuck in a corner and picks out a half bag of clay the color of the red rocks in Sedona with the texture of mud.

Wordless and deliberate, he brings it over, pulls out a chunk the size of a large grapefruit and throws it onto the table permanently covered with a cloth for working clay. Almost in one movement he begins kneading the big soft mass of red clay into the form of a coned seashell, spiraling the dough as if it were one with his body. Masaki is a human silkworm or spider using itself as the medium for its artistry as the rhythm of his hands opening and closing, turning and twisting, pour forth his creation in process. He kneads the clay for several minutes as we try to take in the method and the movement. In final form the clay now looks like a long birdnest or a beehive, a container filled with potentiality.

"See. That's all there is to it," he says. "Let's see you do it."

My husband and I look at each other nervously, then take handfuls of clay from the plastic bag and do our awkward rendition of his dance, mashing the foreign red substance into the table. "Maybe you could just fold and push down," Masaki suggests to my husband who is unclear how to proceed. "To get out the air, so it doesn't blow up in the oven," he adds gently. I have a slight idea of the kneading process, since I used to make bread when my children were small, but my kneaded clay still bears no resemblance to the universal.

After several more minutes of folding and kneading we are sort of set. Masaki turns toward the wheel and we watch him throw the beehive of clay almost into the center of the concentric lines of the metal plate. He begins to pound the clay sideways and down into the silver-gray spinning instrument in a hard, drumbeat rhythm, as his foot finds a pulse of its own. "You keep your arms balanced on your knees, like this, see," he informs us. We can actually see his energy move and his power lock as his legs, back, shoulders and arms become a single organism, a solid force behind his hands which are then free to play and experiment with his medium. He is sensually at ease with the clay, and his assumed control allows him to pull the clay up like a snake charmer until it is a thin, narrow rope over a foot high, and he then easily returns it down with his flattened thumbs. Then it is up in the air again and then dramatically coiled and dangling over the edge, a sidewinder beginning a night journey.

"No problem in recentering," I observe, as he drops the coil to a less heady level and flattens it out.

"So, are you centered in your life?" Masaki asks, deadpan except for a hint of levity in his eyes through his glasses.

I shake my head rapidly. "No. Of course not."

"Then why do you need to be centered in your art? I am not centered, so my clay is not. I enjoy my human experience." At this he takes his thumbs and presses deep down into the wide center to open the clay, creating a cavity that reveals its range and insides. All this while Masaki has been intermittently pouring red-brown water over his hands and on the machinery, to keep the piece fluid and to prevent his skin from tearing on the clay and wheel that rapidly dry out in the fast moving air. Libations to the wheel, to the clay, to movement, I think, as I watch Masaki raise and lower the living piece of earth and easily demonstrate how to make vases and bottles and hourglass shapes and to finally open and spread the clay thinner and thinner, into a red-brown open platter, spirals from the inside turning out wider and wider to a foot and a half in diameter.

Masaki is right, I realize. This exquisite piece is not perfectly centered on the wheel. It is instead centered in imperfection and individuality.

I murmur in respect and admiration, and he slices the magnificent platter off the wheel, not to hand it to us to check out or to gift it to us, but to smash it down into the solid brown shape he began with.

Masaki's voice reaches into our stunned silence, "You have to learn detachment," he states and then adds, embarrassing us: "I don't give away my work."

Up to that moment and afterward, for hours freely given, Masaki patiently and generously—clear that he was not to be paid for it—gave to us of his time and expertise. As I linked my arms stiffly to my knees and spun the silver wheel with my awkward gait, feeling for the first time the immense joy of silken clay easily pouring through my hands, he guided and affirmed, watched and encouraged, coalescing his energy into a strong nurturing power that rang through him and resonated inside of me. He continued to stay present in a gentle, paternal way as my husband took his turn, steadily learning the qualities of the material and his own strength and balance, and he remained by us until 3:00 in the morning when we felt we had some small intimation of someday being able to control the extraordinary medium. Masaki then unobtrusively moved on.

Late into the night, finally arrived in the small room at the art center that has just become my home, I replay the lessons I have learned and offer silent thanks to Masaki. I drift off to sleep one step closer to acceptance of my own and the world's inadequacies and paradoxes. In the turns and twists of the earthy medium I am befriending, I continue to study detachment, generosity, and living off-center.

My Clothes

(Prompt: My Clothes)

Barbara Link

enjoy a second domestic period.
The long soft grays like nonfat milk,
        thin pale nourishment;
the linens glow lilac, mauve, dusty rose and vanilla cream;
the winter plaids meet for lunch,
        the brown croc loafers skip dessert;
the black and whites play chess, tango when home alone.
I bring home a stranger,
        maraschino cherry, knit, sleek as a pimp's hair,
        demanding something strappy for my
        feet and undies that peel like sunburned skin.
The grays turn cool as silver spoons,
        the linens flutter limp wrists to pale foreheads,
        the plaids fart like slide trombones,
        the black and whites trump their race cards
        and rhumba on the face of the
        red dress.

∽

The Fabulous History of the Mayor of Silverfish

(Prompt: The Sign Painter and Jake's Place)

Tom Fante

*O*ur town's road sign painter, Albert, used to come to my street every other year. I was just a boy then. I remember that he was good with backgrounds, red was his favorite color, but he couldn't spell. For several months, my street had a STUP sign, till people complained that drivers were ignoring it. People tell me Albert wasn't always that way. He got dumb by getting hit on the head. A lamppost globe fell on him while painting, and the concussion caused him to become an idiot. Sometimes he forgot to bring his paint. He muttered and waved his hand, up and down, brush or no brush, but the good-hearted city-streets division, being union, couldn't let him go. That's job security, some folks said; others argued it was the "Idiot's Full Employment Act," but isn't an idiot entitled to earn a living too? That question has since been answered.

The sign painter's full name is Albert Hopper and he's still at it. He was born right here in Silverfish and everybody knows him. He has a small, bald, egg-shaped head, barrel chest, thick arms, reedy legs, pale freckles, and yellow teeth. He is gentle, happy, sloppy, and always smells like latex paint. He smiles a lot, and that endeared him to townspeople over his predecessor, who wasn't an idiot, but had a vindictive streak and hated his job. The predecessor once replaced a stop sign and didn't bother to report that it was all but hidden behind a tree; "Not my job," he said, after the accident.

Albert wasn't much in high school, even before he turned idiot. Some people claim he never went to school at all. "That bump on Albert's head was a fork in the road of his life and ours," I heard a man say. Albert slid rapidly from mediocrity into idiocy and stayed there. Strangely, he got happier after the knock on his head. Today, he sings and dances as he paints. The sight of Albert before a road sign, brush in hand, humming a popular tune is now so common as to pass without rude comment. Albert's happiness is infectious, and today people look forward to catching sight of him. He is considered our good omen.

When Albert sings, he waves his brush like a conductor's baton; it looks like he's leading an orchestra. Lately he's taken to painting at night and painting the trees, but what does it matter if he has no paint?

Once, the City Streets Division tried to get rid of him. Their plan was clever. They promoted him to Road Painter, Class A and sent him down to the corner of Main Street and Broadway to paint crosswalks. Maybe they were hoping a car would hit him. The intersection is one of the busiest in town. Instead, Albert took out his biggest brush and began waving it. Suddenly the swarm of erratic cars assumed a more organized character, and traffic began to flow smoothly. The number of accidents went down; people's lives were saved. The phenomenon was remarked upon, and editorials written in our local newspaper. It was just after this that someone wrote a Letter to the Editor saying that if an idiot could save lives at a dangerous downtown intersection, where nothing had previously worked, what wonders might he do if elected mayor? The idea was treated as a joke, but Albert's name was placed on the ballot.

It was at this point that fate took a turn, as the saying goes. There's a bar in Silverfish called Jack's where people used to go after work. It was a rude dive that had gotten quite the bad reputation over the years because the people who drank there formed a group they called the Halloween Wrecking Crew. His or her purpose (as far as anyone could determine) was to make every night Halloween night. The only exception to this rule was Halloween night itself. That night they stayed home and turned off all the lights or went to a G-rated movie. They objected to the way Halloween had been turned into the exclusive preserve of little kids and apple-pie, pink-cheeked, middle-class matrons, who'd ruined its devilish reputation.

Since every other night of the year was Halloween night, they kept closets full of costumes at Jack's, and after "getting looped" (as they liked to call it) they got dressed up and ventured into the night dressed as demons or angels, thieves or priests, cops, druids, or whatever. The only rule was that they had to act the opposite of what their costumes might seem to imply. Thus, we citizens of Silverfish experienced a rash of pranks by cops and tricks by priests, while demons escorted children and old women across crowded streets and doffed horns as a gesture of respect. Angels were seen soaping windows or pouring molasses on sidewalks causing pedestrians shoes to get gummy. Then they laughed merrily and scampered away while a solicitous demon arrived to assist the person through the mess.

This behavior had gone on for so long that people's views got a bit warped. Cops and priests were universally detested, and every angelic statue in town had either been defaced or toppled. Everywhere devil's heads were scratched on walls and gargoyles adorned with garlands of flowers. There was a large statue of Satan in our Town Square, only his horns were blunt, and instead of the wings of a bat, he had wings of painted white feathers. Conversely, the statue of the Archangel Michael at St. Philemon's Church had acquired a set of bat wings and white fangs protruded from his marble mouth. Our morals were on a downhill slide.

Who could you trust? A vampire angel or a reformed and newly-feathered demon? Groups of citizens formed in support of either personage, only to dissolve and form again. Supporters switched sides and members of the Halloween Wrecking Crew were behind it. Some long-time members of the group suddenly seemed to utterly abhor everything they once stood for. They preached on street corners and bellowed from pulpits excoriating and denouncing—themselves. Our town needed a return to simple values, that's what most people thought, but who was going to lead us?

Not everyone was in favor of Albert: Elect an idiot to office? That didn't seem to make much sense. But as the days passed before the election, a general mood took hold that, in order to get anything done, it might be better to elect an idiot and see what happened than elect someone else and watch him turn into an idiot. The election pitted Albert against the incumbent who'd done nothing over the years but get elected to office. He'd built up a sizeable campaign fund by taking up collections at places like Jack's, but his money didn't help him.

Albert won the crucial election. Today, he waves his paintbrush in City Hall and raps it like a gavel, calling the City Council to order. Gradually the swarm of crazy proposals has assumed a more organized character, and the number of citizen complaints gone way down. Albert has set a fine example; even in his new position, he didn't stop painting road signs. Our city filled two positions for the price of one.

People with business proposals or seeking permits, and people with ideas for new city ordinances roll them up on pieces of paper held by rubber bands and place them inside an empty paint can that Albert takes with him everywhere. Sometimes Albert loses the contents or forgets to empty the can before filling it with paint, but just as often he pulls something out of his can and presents it to the City Council. The public's business seems to get done, and much faster too, than under the old administration, which submitted all proposals to the City Planning Department for consideration.

Albert's solution to the problem of the Halloween Wrecking Crew was arrestingly simple: Jail anyone wearing a costume even on Halloween. It didn't matter what you were for or against. True, we had to give up our freedom to dress as some would like. Now everyone must wear a jacket, a long-sleeved white shirt, slacks, and a tie. Everything else is a costume. No scary films are allowed in our local theater. Our cable station broadcasts only G-rated movies.

At first there was a giddy sense that with Albert in charge, the good old days were about to return. That's what people said. It's not every town that's smart enough to put a real idiot in charge, they said, but no one knew what the Halloween Wrecking Crew was going to do. Would they counterattack?

Their attack came last Sunday, but it proved the undoing of the Crew. Opposing members fought it out all over town with sermons, speeches, and vituperation. Believers in the ideals of the Halloween Wrecking Crew ultimately prevailed in the melee against the Wrecking Crew members, who opposed their own group. With this victory, no one is quite sure if the Halloween Wrecking Crew still exists, since it is now composed entirely of non-members who, while they supported its aims, have no intention of joining. Meanwhile the defeated faction is said to be licking its wounds and planning to retake the name, though it is utterly opposed to everything it stands for.

Arresting the lot of them came as a relief not only to the people of our town, but, to tell the truth, to the members of the Crew itself, who were exhausted by their internecine war. Today, if you want to cause trouble, you go somewhere else; if you want to have fun, you go somewhere else; if you want to see a scary movie, you go somewhere else; if you want to dress weirdly, you do it elsewhere. Not everyone is happy with our town's being run by an idiot, but we all sleep more soundly at night.

☙

Chapter 6

Feedback Drives Improvement

Virginia Kidd

I AM LOST IN THE JUNGLE, alone and vulnerable, and I can hear the hyenas circling.

That's what it feels like, anyway, when I am about to receive feedback on my writing. I wrote what the prompt inspired. I even—a little hesitantly—read it aloud. Now the group is stepping up to tell me whether my prose conveyed the depth and charm of my fantasies or resembled a classified ad for a chain saw.

Receiving feedback on our writing is ticklish. We write without knowing how a reader will respond. Appropriate feedback can give us helpful insight into how we come across—where our writing is strong and where it could use some buttressing. However, the wrong kind of feedback can stifle a sensitive writer.

It is also a challenge to give feedback. When a writer shares her or his work with us, how do we convey our impressions without demoralizing the author? A friend of mine (who was not in a group) wrote about her disabled daughter and the challenges of trying to give her the best life possible. When she showed her work to friends who were not writers, one offered only the observation that a word was misspelled; another suggested she should write about the good times instead of what she had written; a third began discussing her own daughter. No one really heard what the author was trying to say, and the group's feedback did not help her. In contrast, I recently wrote a piece that lay like a dead fish on the plate until the people in my group helped me identify what was wrong. That was good feedback.

A group must decide what kind of feedback to give. Telling a group member what works about what she has written can give her encouragement. However, receiving solely positive feedback does not help us overcome weaknesses; we also need suggestions about how to make our characters come alive, our descriptions shine, our dialogue leap off the page. Good feedback can help us hone a particular area or tell us what part of our writing needs attention.

Beginning writers generally operate at a different level than experienced ones; they may need encouragement more than critical input. Experienced writers, however, need the group to help them improve. Sometimes, the best approach is to ask authors what kind of feedback they want; or as the author, you can ask the group to focus on whatever concerns you, such as level of conflict or character development. In our group, we sometimes bring in material we have worked on outside the meetings. In these cases, while compliments are nice, what we really need is feedback on how to get the material to a publishable level.

The conditions for writing also make a difference in feedback. Timed writings are for practice, scrawled out by hand to the distractions of coffee grinders, screeching milk steamers, vague background music, and the monotonous Bible thumping of a woman at the next table attempting religious conversion of the people sitting with her. Readers of pieces written under these conditions should not expect to find the polish of a manuscript that has been edited and revised.

Sometimes special feedback techniques may be used. On occasion Natalie Goldberg asks listeners to restate, exactly, whatever stood out for them in a piece of writing. This stresses the importance of vital detail. Another technique is to exchange written copy and ask reviewers to highlight all the places that grabbed them. Other writing instructors commonly ask authors to simply listen to the group response, making no comments, taking in what is helpful and seeing that which is as a reader's response.

One area that can be difficult when giving feedback is responding to writing that is in a form or genre that the reader does not follow. What is essential in nonfiction, for example, may be irrelevant in fiction. Sometimes this can cause feedback that is confusing or destructive. For instance, poetry often relies on very indirect phrasing and imagery to convey its message. To provide feedback based on standards of clarity is not helpful. Mysteries often leave areas unanswered at the outset; to direct authors to explain a situation right away is to take away the format of a mystery.

Feedback does more than simply help the author to whom it is directed. Group members learn from hearing others' feedback. What strikes listeners about Teresa's description of the Monterey seashore can guide what I write about the Sacramento River. Hearing how positively listeners responded to

Anne's description of Thanksgiving is a model of how to create a family scene. The group's comments about writing are lessons for all of us in the group.

Over time, good feedback builds trust. In effect, when we share our writing, we are opening up to our group members and trusting that they will help strengthen our work. Such trust is one of the keys of maintaining the group over time. When we give and receive honest feedback designed to help one another, we build good relationships as well as good writing.

The basic goals of a writing group are to help the members uncover their creative depths, develop their talent, and gain the confidence to share their work. If you are giving feedback, keep the goals in mind, and if you are receiving feedback, remember how hard it can be to say exactly the right thing and appreciate the efforts of your group members struggling to help you.

Chapter 7

Give It a Voice:
More Writing Examples

Anne Da Vigo

ON APRIL 9, 2001, one of us drew this prompt out of the box: "What I Always Wanted Most Was…" I wrote about red shoes. I had last owned a pair when Gerald Ford was president. They were red leather wedgies. I had worn them with a pair of bell-bottomed jeans and a white gauze shirt, and I'd looked so rockin'.

The writers group wrote for 20 minutes. Mine was about a little girl looking in a shoe store window yearning for a pair of red tennies. Her mother said she couldn't afford them. After I read mine aloud, I told the group I loved red shoes but always went for the practical black or brown because I could get more use out of them. I couldn't afford red.

Tom Fante tilted his head and gave me his trademark skeptical look. "You mean, in the last 30 years, even though you're a highly-paid state employee, you've never been able to afford a pair of red shoes?"

Ooops. I'd been caught in my "sad-little-me" story. Before the next meeting I bought a pair of Aerosole clogs with bright red stretch material across the arch. I wore them on Monday night and strutted around in them. Since then I've purchased a pair of backless, tooled-leather Italian shoes with high heels and pointed toes. Red.

That's how a group works with writing, too. Once you voice something aloud, that thought has weight and becomes a force in the world.

This part of the book is another section that includes a group of longer pieces written from a prompt and read aloud in our usual format, then expanded and polished. Virginia Kidd, in "My First Grade Teacher," sketched a six-year-old girl that may be the central figure of a novel. Barbara's take on "Bringing Home the Fiancee" was molded into a story that eventually was published in a literary magazine. I took the prompt, "Someone's Routine is Interrupted and his or her Life is Changed Forever" and created the opening scene of a book.

You may have a catalog of reasons why you can't expand one of your twenty-minute group-writing efforts into a finished piece. Your boss is squeezing you to get a project finished. You are the designated soccer team chauffeur. You have an appointment with the plumber. That's okay. We all have our own list of reasons.

The power of the group is in the speaking of your writing. Once you read it out loud, the writers keep leading you back to your aspirations. Someone remembers the twenty-minute piece you wrote about the little tomboy kicking the dust in her grandmother's backyard or the horny divorcee driving her 1976 Volkswagon down the freeway with a chilled glass of tequila sunrise between her legs. Your listeners want to know more.

Your loyal group members prod and nudge you. Once you've made a first try at polishing it, they offer to read it and give you generous feedback Your piece builds momentum. Someone spots a new magazine that publishes the same type of work. Another member saw a similar piece, but not as good. A third person digs out an editor's business card.

In speaking your writing to the world, the world aligns on your dreams of being a writer and makes them real.

My First Grade Teacher
by Mary Margaret Mendlebrine

(Prompt: My First Grade Teacher)

Virginia Kidd

My first grade teacher is Ms. Curtis and she is mean as pus. She makes me sit right by her desk and write the alphabet on straight lines and count blocks and add and not dance at all unless she says, and she never says because she thinks you can only dance when you hear music instead of anytime you want. I told her if she would dance, people would make music, and she said I was giving her gray hair. At first I thought she was thanking me. I think anybody'd rather have gray hair than that fuzzy red stuff on her head. It just pokes out from her face in wiggly curls like she doesn't even brush it. And she has freckles all over her face, too, and she never wants to do art, especially not on the walls, so they are all white and ugly when we could have walls with the most beautiful flowers in the universe on them, and elephants too. I make very good elephants. The secret to making good elephants is to make them very big, so big you don't have to draw their heads or trunks or those white things that stick out the front. The good thing about elephants is they don't have spots. Giraffes are really hard to draw because of the spots. I made a frog that was stepped on by an elephant, but Ms. Curtis called it a spot and said I had spilled my chocolate milk. She made me wipe it up. She's just mean as pus. I'll be glad to be in the second grade. I hope Ms. Curtis gets fired and has to go somewhere and teach only boys, who are putrid pieces of puke.

Passages

(Prompt: Childbirth Stories)

Shauna L. Smith

Round tummy
Pumpkin coach
        carrying
Its passenger
Through rapid evolutions.

Curving stem
Swirling through warm waters
Flowering ears and heart,
Leafing fingers and toes,

Curly tendril
Filtering nourishment,
Eyelids and follicules, membranes,
        filling with
Shifting substance,
Embodying wet spirit.

Round belly,
Pumpkin coach.
How empty your
Red-orange sphere
When its once tiny passenger
        emerges,
Floating away to its new home.

∞

The Westin: A Fictionalized Account

(Prompt: Isolate the Senses)

Deb Marois

*S*elect a crowded place: Community-Building Conference, Westin Hotel, Seattle, Washington

1. Your character can only smell, touch, and taste
A rough-skinned hand grasps mine, gently pulling me towards the shuttle van door. I reach down, my free hand clumsily landing on a man's slight shoulder, round yet with a determined hardness underneath. I am guided down onto one large step and am finally standing upright. I breathe in the moist air flavored with afternoon sprinkles, exhaust from waiting taxis, and cigarettes from sidewalk smokers. The van driver gives my hand one last squeeze as I press crinkled bills into his waiting palm and turn toward my next guide.

We enter the hotel. I hear the faint vacuum seal as the doors close against the outside world. As we progress along a corridor, the air becomes increasingly cooler and it would be fresh if it ever circulated beyond the building's interior. In the elevator, I am pressed between the wall and a tall woman whose Wrigley Spearmint-scented breath mixes with Jovan Musk above my head. Within moments, the dip in my stomach tells me we've come to a stop and bodies brush lightly past me on their way to registration.

2. Your character can only hear now.
"Right this way ma'am." The bellhop's voice is surprisingly deep. It sounds like it comes from a place hidden inside, a place that keeps secrets. The woman ahead of us in line recounts her latest travel trauma to her fellow traveler. "I've been on the red-eye all night, delayed once in Chicago, and I'm done in. These people better have my room ready."

A constant buzz of fragments of conversation along with upbeat, smooth jazz piped into the lobby ensures that none of us are for one moment left in silence. No chance for random thoughts to bubble to the surface, or for aloneness to set in. "Next please," a woman's no-nonsense, efficiency-driven voice calls out across the throng. "Name? Confirmation number? Smoking or non?" She doesn't miss a beat between question, answer, and computer entry. Then she's on to the next spiel: "Are you familiar with all our amenities? There is a self-service mini-bar in your room and movies on demand. The TV guide is on Channel 2. Spa, pool, and fitness center on the Fourth Floor. Pool and spa close at ten, fitness center open twenty-four hours." Someone behind me says, "The last time I was at the Westin, I was outside protesting the WTO."

3. Now your character can only see.
The hotel clerk wears her auburn hair twisted into a tight bun; the strands lay sleek against her scalp. Pressed creases on her starched white blouse appear flawlessly in all the right places. She wears a small American flag pinned to her lapel, its red, white, and blue trimmed in gold. Her Timex keeps track to the second. In the lobby, I'm surrounded by a colorful assortment of people, clothing, and luggage. A short, red-bearded man sporting a curly Afro hurries by, dragging an oversized plaid suitcase. He wears a silky tie-dyed sarong and purple paisley shirt. A tall woman with chocolate skin, tight braids, and bright red lipstick glides by, her gauzy tunic trailing behind. People cluster together on comfortable couches and overstuffed chairs, sipping the perennial Seattle coffee or the occasional glass of wine. Glass cases are strategically placed along the mezzanine. They house a variety of expensive art, glassware, and jewelry.

4. Dialogue only
"Why are you telling me this now?" I demand of the conference organizer. He towers over me; the male-pattern baldness on the top of his forehead catches the light of the lobby chandeliers and shoots a reflected glare back towards me.

"I'm sorry Ms. Liberty, I really am. I know you've prepared to present a two-hour workshop, but unfortunately we have no choice but to alter the agenda. Please understand."

"Well I don't understand. This is supposed to be a conference focused on community building." I stress the last two words, my tight voice rising at least two levels in pitch. "And now you're bumping me for the sake of a politico who is doing nothing more that seizing the opportunity to advance his anti-terrorist agenda?" Richard watched me with a wary eye, his jaw slack and face expressionless. "What has that guy ever done to build community? He stirs up controversy wherever he goes. There are many people who consider him dangerous—a threat to civil rights at best. I won't even state the worst-case scenario. What are you people thinking?"

"Look," Richard sighs. "I've done the best I can. I answer to people. Higher-ups who expect me to make them look good."

"They're not looking too good from where I stand," I interject.

He sighs again, drawing breath from deep in his belly and expelling it in my direction. A faint odor of coffee escapes despite the spearmint breath mints that promised instant freshness. "I'm sorry to hear you say that, ma'am. We're doing the best we can to accommodate all conference attendees. There's nothing more I can do about it. Perhaps we can work together again in the future."

"Don't bet on it," I spit out. "As a matter of fact, I have a good mind to organize a protest. I hear there are some folks here with experience in that sort of thing. They're sure to be some more interested in integrity than politeness. I guess your higher-ups will look real good then."

∽

Water's Edge

(Prompt: Someone's Routine Is Interrupted and his or her Life Is Changed Forever)

Anne Da Vigo

The doorbell rang. Christine Meyers drew the safety razor down her son's cheek, mowing a strip of thick shaving cream off his skin.

She called over her shoulder, "Danny, get that, will you?" She tilted Everett's chin toward the bathroom ceiling so she could scrape a clump of stiff whiskers off his neck. His vulnerable Adam's apple bobbed as he swallowed.

"Mustache. I want a mustache. Like Gable. " Everett formed the words slowly, his mouth working them like a fist forming a ball of dough. His blue eyes glinted.

"No way, you Romeo." Christine rubbed her upper lip to hide a grin. One hand propped on her thigh, she bent her knees so her face was level with his as he sat on the closed toilet seat lid. Like this, when his features were relaxed, he reminded her of Joel when they first met. She felt a rush of love and sadness.

"Sideburns," Everett said.

"Too late."

The bell rang again, impatiently, as if a finger were stabbing at the button. "Danny, get off the computer and answer the damn door." She turned on the hot water faucet and flipped the razor back and forth under the stream. Drops splashed onto her white cotton tank top and she fanned the hem to dry it.

With a navy blue towel draped over her palms, she cradled Everett's face, drying it and wiping away the last scraps of shaving cream. His skin glowed, pink and healthy. Her fingers lingered on his cheekbone. When he was freshly shaved, he looked like any other twenty-one-year-old.

The bell again. "All right, all right." Christine felt the ache of irritation at the points of her jaw. Danny must have his headphones on while he did his homework. She entertained a moment's fantasy of throwing Danny's computer onto the patio from his second-story bedroom window. She tossed the towel on the tiled counter, then cupped Everett's shoulder. His thin bones felt like a handful of chicken wings. "I'll be right back."

She trotted down the hall, her bare feet whispering on the carpet. The stairs were dim, and from the steps she could see a bar of late afternoon sun slashing across the entryway. At the bottom, she paused. Her pulse pounded in her ears. A man's silhouette was outlined against the etched glass in the door.

Heat smacked her face when she opened it. Her pupils contracted in the brutal light. He was in his late 50s, the bald dome of his head shiny with sweat, long hairs from his thick eyebrows nearly obscuring his eyes. He wore an olive green suit with the jacket straining against the single button over his stomach. The acrid odor of cigarettes clung to him like his own personal pocket of air. How many cigarettes did he smoke a day to reek that badly?

"M'am." His voice was odd—high and soft, where she'd been expecting low and phlemy. "M'am, are you Mrs. Christine Meyers?"

She nodded, suddenly, sickeningly, certain of what he was going to say.

"I'm from the county coroner's office."

The heat and smell of cigarette smoke made her nauseated. "Joel is dead," she said.

He nodded. "His vehicle ran off the levee and into the Sacramento River. Divers recovered his remains about an hour ago." He slipped a handkerchief from his jacket pocket and patted the moisture on his forehead. "There was a passenger. A young woman."

∽

Dusk

(Prompt: The Best Time of Day, the Worst Time of Day)

Virginia Kidd

*D*usk came upon Meg the way age does, not really out of the blue, but still a surprise. She rested against a redwood fence post and watched the pale light far across the meadow make a silhouette of the Tetons. Evening's steadily colder wind left pinpoint tingles on her cheeks. The heavy, grassy perfume filled her with melancholy. Absently, she brushed away a swarm of gnats, then dug in her jeans for Chapstick and smeared it across her lips.

Dusk was peaceful, like giving up. It was too late now for her "to do" list, too late to respond to demanding phone calls and insistent e-mails, too late to pretend she would make evening plans, too late for leaning toward someone across a white linen table cloth watching candlelight flicker through chardonnay.

It was another tuna salad night, dinner with Frazier or the Third Rock crew. She lingered, waiting, she told herself, for Venus.

Dusk slid away as it had come, slowly and suddenly, both at once. The night chill blew down her open collar. Gnats returned with allies, determined to nest in her hair. The fence post dug into her palm, gouging a splinter into her lifeline.

Still she lingered, unwilling to face the cold night waiting indoors.

∞

Grief Comes Calling

(Prompt: Describe a Character or a Room as Seen through a Window)

Deb Marois

*S*he dashes across the rough, short pile rug. Her hair is slicked back; droplets gently shake loose from curled ringlets. Lunging toward the counter, her body obscures her objective. She begins to pace across the kitchen, a phone lodged against her ear. Her mouth moves, silent conversation incomprehensible through the double-paned glass. The light from the kitchen is harsh and contrasts sharply with the living room, bathed in shadows. Her form appears distinct and solid–blocking the last rays of sunlight fading behind cloud-covered sky.

Suddenly, she sinks to the floor. Her knees rest near her chin and within moments, her head drops, her dark hair shielding the world from her expression. Outside, the night gathers around the window, leaving her huddled figure illuminated within the private haven she calls home.

She reaches slowly above her head, stretching to drop the receiver in its cradle and continues to sit motionless, hugging her knees and then, slowly, she begins to rock back and forth. A shrill sound akin to animal screeching pierces the night air, escaping through the glass. A sympathetic tabby nudges her clasped hands, pushing its nose under her fingers. She jerks away and drags herself to her feet. Shuffling across the darkened living room and clutching the railing, she slowly disappears up the stairs.

෨

Lemon Dessert

(Prompt: Show How a Good Deed Can Backfire)

Barbara Link

Shaking the heavy paper sack, I emptied the last of the granulated sugar into the egg yolks. With my wire whisk, I beat the mixture and set it over medium heat until it bubbled and turned a light yellow color. Then I added a piece of butter the size of a small egg and juice from three lemons.

Just this morning I'd harvested the yellow fruits from my small Meyer lemon tree. A whole year of growing and it produced only three of the special lemons that I prized for tart—but not sour—lemon flavor. I had let the lemons hang on the tree until they were squishy and full of juice.

This promised to be a great lemon meringue pie. The crust flaky and golden brown, the filling pale and lemony and the meringue high and white with peaks of toasted brown—the pie of all pies. The one that would capture the blue ribbon at the California State Fair, the pie that would cause angry words to melt like August snow, the pie that would send men to their knees with declarations of love and pleas for marriage.

I argued with myself over the method of delivery: place it carefully in a large white dress box with a yellow bow, leave it at the door like a May basket, ring the bell and dash away. No, I'd slip inside Kurt's apartment and leave it shining high on my crystal cake plate. When he arrived after his shift at Rainbo Bread, he'd smell warm lemon then spy the meringue delight cooling on his kitchen island.

I allowed myself one snaky lick on the rubber scraper to be sure of the ambrosia-like flavor, made my delivery, and waited for the phone, the doorbell, the cheering crowd. This was a home run, a bases-loaded, home run pie.

Back at home, I peered out my bathroom window by standing on the john and craning my neck in just the right way to watch his parking space. The Chevy truck arrived at 6:23 as usual. I'd get the call any minute now. I paced from the kitchen to the living room to the bedroom, all of twenty-five feet round trip. I dusted, I wiped, I scraped, I cleaned the bottom drawer of the refrigerator. I threw away the brown, soggy lettuce, discovered a Fuji apple that was still firm, and ate three wilted baby carrots. I resisted the urge to vacuum, afraid I would miss the doorbell or phone.

An hour later I checked the parking lot. The truck was gone. The phone rang and I jumped off my perch on the john and landed hard on my right ankle. I stumbled to the phone.

"Hel-lo." I panted.

"Hey, Carla, can you give me a lift?"

"Where…where on earth are you?" I was impatient for my payoff.

"At the vet's. That damn fool Cheyenne ate something bad. I don't know what—something yellow. Those labs will gobble anything. He's barfing sick and I have to get him home and my truck won't start!"

☞

Water

(Prompt: Personify an Object in the Kitchen)

Shauna L. Smith

I am water, an object, a subject, I am in everything. No appliance in your kitchen can exist without me. I am everywhere, glossy and translucent, giving movement and life with my co-creator, electricity. Without us, every piece of acrylic, lead, steel, copper, plastic, is silent and still.

I am the voice and throat of your kitchen, which is the sacrum of your family's soul. I flow onto your fine glasses and mismatched china, between the prongs of your forks, sit and spin in the centers of your spoons, swirl paintings in your sink, I bubble up in your pans and whistle in your kettles. I scald your vegetables and grain, slake your thirst. I configure into cubes and chips of ice.

I clean your clothing filled with sweat, and chocolate, and blood. I pour through your pipes into a silver spray, hot and cold and in between, and pour over your hands like a lover, exploring every cell and line, feeling you under and over, around me. I see and smell the core of you as you swallow me and I follow your most private curves, knowing for a brief moment every note of your most secretive song.

cఖ

The Mystery of Lake Baby Blue

(Prompt: Write about a Color)

Tom Fante

A cold wind blows over the desert. In gusts it slips below the canvas top of the covered wagon and finds its way inside. Each time she feels the cold, Helena Santos shivers and pulls her coat tighter. As the wagon rolls over the hard ground, she lies inside on a blanket trying to sleep while up front her father dozes at the reins.

"Helena!"

She turns but does not rise at the familiar sound of Jedediah's voice.

"Were you dreaming?" Jedediah asks.

"I dreamed I was flying."

"Why try to sleep when we are on the move?"

"Where are we?"

"We're coming to a lake."

Helena lifts herself on one arm and looks under the canvas at her brother.

"I see an island in the middle of a lake," Jedediah says.

Jedediah is wearing a red flannel shirt and blue cotton pants. His pants are tucked into his worn leather boots. For effect, he sports a frayed yellow scarf and a gray felt hat. The hat is better suited to a man who works in an office. Helena thinks how like a boy it is to always be playing at life. He loves pretending to be a pioneer.

"I'm all right, Jedediah."

"All right," he echoes.

Helena falls back and hears the sound of Jedediah's horse galloping to the lake. He is going to be the first to reach the shore. Rocks beneath the wagon's iron-rimmed wheels roughly jostle her. Helena stares at the canvas covering as it pitches. The early morning desert air smells of flowers.

The rest of the Santos party is excited. Helena hears them yelling to each other.

"A lake! It's a blue lake!" little Paul says.

"It's there," Marguerite says. "An island in the middle of the lake!"

It's all so dull, Helena thinks, so dreary. There's no chair to sit in and no bed in which to sleep. She hates the bleakness of this desert crossing.

"Helena," Martin says.

He has dropped back from his position in front to be beside the wagon. He is their guide. The lake is all before them; it fills the horizon. Helena does not answer him.

"Don't taste the water till I get there," he yells to Jedediah.

But no one is listening. The tip of the sun has risen over the lake and its light glances off the surface turning its color from blue to blazing silver.

I hate this, Helena thinks.

"Have you got up Helena?"

It is her father, Victor, talking to her from the driver's side of the wagon.

Helena lies on her blanket and the wagon bumps along. She feels her shoulders as they bounce and fall on the wood floor. She has thin arms and legs and a long neck. At sixteen, she's still scrawny, but she's tougher than she pretends. She is sturdy enough for a journey like this. Martin called her a little stick once and she got so angry she spit at him. Now he calls her a spitfire.

"You've got quite the temper," Martin said. Helena could tell he was impressed. She's not a stick; she's a reed and the right man will play her like a pipe and she will be music to him. She has small hand and strong sinuous fingers. She has artist's fingers.

Victor is thinking. Why doesn't Marguerite take their daughter more in hand? He needs to pay heed to his sons. They are growing up wild. Little Paul skips on the hard ground beside the plodding oxen. He picks up smooth stones and throws them at the birds. Jedediah is far ahead now and almost out of sight. Neither one listens to him anymore. My little girl is such a strange creature, Victor thinks. She's like her mother. Both scrawny, but they are so damn stubborn! Helena has a burning gaze, as if she could see inside things, but what does she really see when she looks?

Victor lifts his whip and cracks it over the head of an ox to move it left before him. He looks at Martin whose lips are moving while his eyes are closed. He looks like a man praying, Victor thinks.

The oxen stir up a cloud of powdery white dust as they walk. The wagon is in the dry bed of a creek that rolls into the lake ahead. The dust is the last obstacle they will face today; they will camp beside the lake. The ground ahead is flat and hard. Last night's full moon made it easy to see the way. In the west, the tops of the mountains stand out like teeth. It was a good idea to travel by night. Now they can rest in the heat and not exert themselves till tomorrow afternoon. There will be another full moon tomorrow night.

Once more the wind picks up and the cold breeze stiffens, but within it is a puff of warm air and the day will be hot, as all the days have been hot since they left the Great Salt Lake. Leaning over his horse, Martin slips in his saddle and almost tumbles off. He rights himself quickly and looks up, but Victor has been intent on his oxen and no one else has seen him. He can hear the sound of a stone knocked by the hoof of his horse as it bounces on a flat rock and the thud it makes as it punches into the powdery dust. They are almost at the lake's edge, but he is hardly interested enough in it to look. He hears a lizard running in a bush nearby and then Helena moans.

"What's the matter with your daughter, Victor?" he asks.

"She has been writing again, that must be it."

"Read something to us," Martin asks.

"When the wagon stops, maybe, but right now, I only get dizzy," Helena answers from inside the wagon.

She has written something in her journal in a long flowing snakelike script: *Grass looks ghostly. I see a single blue pine growing out of some rocks. The moon lights up the clouds. The grass lies down in the breeze. The mountain peaks are white with snow, but this is a dreary place of canyons and more canyons. We are coming to a lake—December 17, 1866.*

"I don't understand," Victor says. "Why not read it to us?"
Such is this strange girl who hides herself from everyone.

Victor Santos can't remember; it's as if he's forgotten why he left the green fields of his Kansas homestead to bring his family west. What was he thinking? And why did he hire a Missouri man as his guide, a man he knows almost nothing about? Now he remembers. He was going to get rich out west, but how? Did he have a plan? He doesn't remember, but it's been a long night and he is tired. He needs to sleep. He will remember tomorrow maybe, or sometime soon.

Helena says nothing, but she is trembling. Somewhere in the distance there is the cry of a bird.

"Do you love Martin?" Marguerite asks.

"I just don't know mother," Helena replies.

Victor's rump is sore from the wagon's endless bumping. He thinks with loathing of his flabby, sixty-year-old body gone weak on this last journey.

"Your daughter's not a girl," Martin says. "Is she of age?"

Victor pretends not hear him. He looks at the lake, rubs his eyes and says: "This place reminds me of…" He doesn't finish and his voice trails off.

Better to die than grow old, Martin thinks.
Victor is thinking that he's raised this girl and been in the same house with her for eighteen years, but he still doesn't know her. He's raised a stranger.

Once again a bird cries and from somewhere nearby there is a sound of wings flapping, but no bird rises into the morning sky.

Victor coughs again. It is a dry cough. He has had it from the day they came down out of the mountains west of Denver. It rips through his lungs and sounds like a sheet of paper being torn down the middle.

"Damned bird," he says.

Martin rides over to the wagon.

"Breathe through your nose, if you can," he says. "It's the dust."

Helena is delicate and her feet are too small to walk beside the wagon. She needs to be carried, Martin thinks.

"How old is Helena?" Martin asks.

"You need not concern yourself," Victor replies.

Meanwhile Helena dresses herself in the pitching wagon. She sits on the floor and pulls her dress over her head. She puts on soft boots that cover her ankles and cling to her legs. She looks past her father's head and sees a large white star above the lake. No, it isn't a star; it's the planet Venus, the morning star. Her mother looks back at her from her place beside her husband. Helena's arms have goose bumps and she is shivering. Helena rolls over and stands up, stooping. She walks forward holding on to one side of the wagon. She puts one leg over the bench and then another and she slides between her mother and father.

She is waiting for the bird to cry a third time and knows it will do so, but out of earshot. Now there is a warm wind on her face. In the distance, birds fly spirals over the island in the lake. Suddenly, the wagon passes over a nest of scorpions; back and forth they run and some of them cling to the wheels and try to climb up the legs of the oxen. One by one they drop to the ground and are crushed.

They are beside the shore of the lake and look out at the island. The edge of the lake is shallow and swarming with minnows. There is a smell of something rotten rising out of the water. They can hardly breathe and realize they will need to make camp some distance away. But already Jedediah and little Paul have taken off their clothes and plunged into the brine. They float upon its smooth surface like corks and cry out that the lake is salt, which is why they cannot drown. Martin grasps the lead ox by its ear and steers it away from the lake as Victor reins the team toward a clump of dark green grass. The boys reach down to scoop up the minnows and let them slip through their fingers, wriggling back into the lake. The wind rises once more off the lake and it brings a smell of rotting weeds. They are all disheartened, but too tired to retreat any further.

They sleep in the morning and rise in the afternoon. The sun is bright, but the day has not been as hot as expected. They gather up pieces of wood to build a fire, talking with each other and deciding what to do.

It's so dull, Helena thinks; Marguerite looks at her and smiles. Martin has gone off by himself, but now he returns in a rustle of weeds and scattering small stones with his boots. He reaches the wagon and leans against it. He sees Helena at rest on a blanket beside the wagon. She turns her head to him, and her blue eyes stare at him. Her bare shoulders are white where the sun has not seen them, but her face is tan. She shivers in his glance and looks away at a small scrub pine that is moving in the wind. Martin stands over her with the sun behind so she cannot see his face inside its halo of sunlight.

Then she hears a rustle in the bushes and she laughs. Is it a snake? Her laugh is almost a jeer, or perhaps it is like the tinkling of a tiny bell.

Martin looks at her and smiles. She can see his fine white teeth. He is sweating from his walk and gives off an odor of musk and soil. She does not wish to resist him now, but she will not exist in his shadow.

"I have been dreaming about you," she says.

He kneels down and touches her face, but she shakes her head.

"Not here."

"Helena!"

"My father is calling me," she says.

She gets up suddenly, moving away from Martin's caress and runs to the pine tree. She pushes a branch aside and lets it go as Martin comes after her. It scratches his hand and stings the side of his face. She runs away again and he follows.

She is wearing man's pants and a loose white blouse. She has on her soft boots and she is not afraid to get them dirty. She flies and he follows till she laughs and collapses onto a bed of fine white sand. She seems stunned as he rushes to her side. She looks at him with her wide blue eyes and faints as his lips touch hers. He picks her up and carries her back to her blanket.

"What happened?" Victor asks.

"She fell," Martin replies.

Helena opens her eyes and shakes her head as she comes to.

"You shouldn't run; it's bad for someone as delicate as you," her mother says.

Helena smiles weakly and waves them away.

"Everything is bad for me. Go away, all of you!"

There is such finality in her statement that they all draw back.

"Let me alone, please!"

She goes to sleep on the blanket.

In the afternoon, little Paul wants to visit the island. Little Paul can't go unless his mother takes him. If she goes, Victor must go and if Victor goes, Martin must lead them. There are some dry logs by the shore and Martin binds them to make a raft. Does Helena want to come? No, the island is boring, but she tells them she's just too tired. Jedediah will stay with her and tend to the animals. The sun is falling down the sky to the west and the lake surface gently ripples. The water looks blue and orange in the light, and birds skim inches over its surface. The four of them sit on the raft, one at each corner, and paddle using their hands. The raft slowly moves toward the island. As they recede, they become silhouettes and then they are just little spots.

Jedediah goes to the wagon for some field glasses. He looks through them and hands them to his sister and she looks. They can't see anything because the light of the setting sun is reflected off the water into their eyes. Helena walks to the shore, takes off her boots, and wades into the warm water. She can feel the soft sand between her toes and the minnows nibbling at her ankles.

The night is well advanced when Helena and her brother begin to worry about the rest of her family and Martin. They should have come back right away, but if they delayed too long they may have decided to stay the night on the island and won't return till morning. Jedediah mounts his horse and rides into the lake. He stands up in his saddle and calls out. "Mother! Father!" There is no echo, no answering call. Helena walks back to the wagon, and Jedediah rejoins her. They light a fire because they know it will be visible from the island and if the others are on the water trying to return, they will move in the right direction. They tend the fire till after midnight keeping it bright, but no one returns from the island. The moon has gone down and the stars are shining. There is Orion followed by his dogs. Sirius is the only star Jedediah knows by name, but Helena can recognize Scorpio and its red star, Antares.

They once had a home in Kansas, a white clapboard house placed abruptly in the middle of rich rolling fields of wheat, corn, and oats. Why had they left? It had not been their decision. They remembered the large picture inside the kitchen. It was a picture of green hills somewhere in Kentucky, and there'd been horses and a gentleman in his red coat riding in an ornate carriage with bright brass lanterns. Was that where their people came from? Kansas was their home, not this place lost in a desert beside the shores of a salt lake. Inside the wagon, Helena finds her journal and writes: *Martin and a baby blue lake.*

That's all she writes though the night is half over when she closes the journal. She was dreaming, but awake she is worried about what has become of them. She makes up a bed for herself inside the wagon. Jedediah tends to the oxen and the horses. She falls asleep as he is making a place for himself beneath the wagon. They will wait for tomorrow. They haven't seen any Indians, but that doesn't mean they aren't around. This place could be dangerous. What if the Indians saw the fire? But they haven't seen any Indians; that is a comfort.

In the morning, Helena and her brother can see the island. Birds wheel overhead and skim the surface of the lake. Jedediah is looking at his frail sister. She is such a beauty, he thinks. He loves her livid complexion. He can see her veins like little blue rivers on a paper map. He has protected her all his life. The memory of her illness comes to him; he sees her sick with pneumonia. She got chicken pox and almost died. She had scarlet fever too. Her eyes were sunk into her face, and they all said she would die, but miraculously she got better, again and again. She has reserves of strength, but she doesn't seem well; she remains delicate and frailty has her in its grip, though little by little she is getting her strength back. It seems to him that the pure air of the desert and the sun have done her good.

Jedediah remembers how he and his father met Martin. They rode to town and found him in the stable shoeing his own horse. He'd rather do for himself than pay another man and his sturdy and independent spirit impressed Victor Santos. Jedediah was more concerned with what they did not know about Martin. They did not know what he did to get by. He had an easy way about him, but Jedediah did not trust him and watched him from time to time; it was clear what he desired—Helena. He could not watch Martin all the time, though. It occurred to him that it was the death of his younger sister that sent them flying across the country. Something about that place in Kansas wasn't right. Pearl got sick just before Helena. Both came down with pneumonia and both were at death's door, but poor Pearl had died and Helena recovered. Jedediah thinks of Pearl lying there all glassy-eyed in her midget-sized pine box. It was so plain a resting-place and such a short service. There was little to say because she died so young and they knew only the Lord's Prayer.

Just after sunrise, Jedediah decides that he must go to the island to find out what has become of the rest. He has paced back and forth between the wagon and the tethered oxen. The island is too far for him to swim. He too must build a raft. He tells Helena to stay with the animals, but she refuses. They will go together or not at all. Jedediah lashes three dry, rotten logs together and places Helena atop the raft. Then he gets into the water and, holding the raft with one hand, he propels it slowly by swimming at its side.

The salty water is warm and buoyant.

At about noon they reach the island and crawl ashore. Jedediah drags the raft onto the beach and helps his sister off. They walk along the beach, and then they turn and edge toward the center of the island. There isn't a blade of grass. The island is entirely made of rock and here and there vapors escape from cracks in the ground. Near the center of the island there is a pool of green water. It is hot to the touch and the sides are salt-crusted. There is no sign of anyone. On another part of the island, near the shore, there is a lilac-colored mist that hides everything. They walk into it and find themselves lost. They keep on walking till they reach another shore, but the mist extends out into the lake and they cannot see the mainland. They walk along the beach until gradually the mist gives way to sunlight and they can see the rest of the island. Looking behind them the mist covers everything, so much so that it looks like the sky.

"This is a horrible place," Helena says. "It reminds me of a dream I had while I was sick. I was alone and couldn't find my way home. The world had no shape and ghosts filled the sky. It was as if I knew I was asleep and I couldn't wake up. It was a nightmare that closed around me. I had to hold my breath and swim up to the light. It took all my strength just to wake up!"

Jedediah does not reply as they continue to walk along the shore till they have gone around the island. Nowhere is there a sign of the rest of the family.

"Maybe they left while we were coming here," Jedediah says.

He and his sister return to their raft and reach camp by late afternoon.

On the third day after the disappearance, a storm rises over the lake. A towering white cloud appears suddenly and lightening flashes below it. Birds circle around the edge of the cloud climbing high into the sky. The rumble of thunder reaches their ears and a few fat raindrops fall onto the dust, but the storm stays over the lake and doesn't move to shore. Gradually the thunder subsides and the clouds become wispy and disappear.

"You should ride around the lake," Helena tells her brother. "They must have come ashore somewhere and gotten lost. I'm sure they're walking around the lake to find us, that is the only thing that makes sense. I'll stay here; I'm too tired to move!"

"What will you do while I am gone?" Jedediah asks.

"I'll watch for them and for you and at night I will light a fire."

"Wait for night to light a fire, and then light it about an hour after sunset, but don't let it burn for more than a minute. I will be look for it, but I don't want the Indians to get you."

"What Indians?"

"If there are Indians," Jedediah replies.

After Jedediah has gone Helena puts on a loose-fitting dress and arranges a bed for herself in the wagon. She releases the oxen so they can find food and tethers the horses nearby. She inspects the stock of supplies and looks into the water barrel. There is food for at least two months, but water for only a few days more. They will need to move camp soon. She has some sewing to do and some dreaming and there will be as much time as she wants to write in her journal. She feels joy at being alone at last and free. Her sense of well being returns as she gulps the desert air. She wanders the beach collecting firewood. That night she lights the first fire.

Jedediah lights his fire too and both fires last for just a moment in the darkness. The next day Jedediah comes upon a swift creek of cold fresh water. It is so strong he has difficulty crossing it. It the west he can see the glimmer of snow atop a high mountain range. It must be the Sierra Nevada.

Sunrise comes and he looks at the island through his field glasses. Then sunset once again and he sits down on a log by the shore and rests. He looks up and stares at the island. He thinks for an instant that he sees something there. Maybe it is a light, but just a glimmer, and then it is gone. The night brings on a cold blanket of air that settles over him. There is a brief spark from Helena's fire that runs like a line over the surface of the lake. It is almost as if he can see his sister inside the fire, like the dark place in the middle of a candle flame.

He looks at the beach and gazes up into the sky. It is hazy and only the larger stars can be seen. A fine mist has risen over the lake and water laps the shore in waves two fingers high. He puts his head down and falls asleep in the silence. He is awakened by the sound of a bird flapping its wings. An owl has landed on the limb of a dead tree beside the lake.

He looks into the lake, but all he sees is a white mist over the water. The mist is folded like a robe and as it moves it ripples, like the surface of the water. He closes his eyes and falls asleep.

"Where are you, my son?"

The words echo in his mind, but when he opens his eyes the sky is clear and the mist is gone. He can see the island more clearly in the last of the moonlight. The owl no longer sits on the tree limb. The sky is pink in the east, pregnant with the sun. He sits up and blinks his eyes. He reaches for his canteen and takes a gulp of water.

It is early but if he hurries he can rejoin his sister before the day gets hot. He takes great strides as he walks by the shore. Sometimes he takes a short cut through a shallow pool of water where fish glitter in the bright light. The sand beneath his feet is loose making it difficult for him to walk. He wonders about the fish in the lake. How can they live in such a poisoned pool? Maybe his family and Martin have returned, and he will see them when he makes it back to camp.

Now he is coming. It is late morning and smoke rises from the campsite; Helena must be cooking breakfast. Doesn't she know that smoke in the day is as dangerous as light in the darkness? From afar he sees his sister sitting beside the wagon and staring at the island. Her journal lies unopened in her lap. Is she dreaming? Yes, she is. Helena sees a city with buildings of alabaster on the island in the lake. The streets are paved with mother of pearl. Martin is riding a white horse. He is dressed Mexican-style in an ornate coat with silver buttons that shine in the sun. Victor drives a red carriage with brass lamps; little Paul is sitting beside him holding four black horses with the reins. Marguerite sits in the carriage dressed in black with braces of silver bracelets running up and down both arms. Helena wants to join them, but Jedediah won't let her go. He sees nothing at all because the island is hidden by mist. Helena is alone in her longing; it is said that she named the lake Baby Blue and was the first to tell the lake's story.

The Santos family was never found. One guess is that they drank some of the brackish water and wandered into the desert. Jedediah Santos went to San Francisco and became a bank clerk. Helena stayed in the area for a few years. She worked part-time as a dancer in a saloon in Bishop and called herself Baby Blue Belle. She was famous for her Spider Dance to the music of a tarantella. What we know of the Santos party comes from her journal, which was found in 1899 in a house where she once lived by a miner who gave it to the local historical society. That's where I discovered it, disregarded on a shelf. My story is based upon what she wrote.

Today, if you visit the area, you will see many birds, and owls are common too, at night. There are sudden thunderstorms over the lake, and the shore smells bad from time to time. Scorpions infest parts of the surrounding country. A gray mist occasionally hides parts of the island. There are minnows in the salty water. All that is true and it also seems that no Indians live by the lake; they think it is cursed, except that many years ago, the rock-message people did live here and their disappearance is part of the mystery of things.

❧

Chapter 8

Cross Pollination: Writing Courses and Seminars

Barbara Link

IF WE WERE BEES, would we go to only one flower for nectar? Not if we were smart bees. The same choice is given to writers. And since we are writers, we have many other sources besides our weekly writers group for inspiration, writing teachers, and technical support.

Three in our group, Anne, Virginia and I (at different times) have taken a week-long class given by the University of California, Berkeley Extension called Fiction Intensive. Tom and I have enrolled at American River College for semester-long writing courses. Last April, five members of the group attended a weekend writing/zen workshop given by Natalie Goldberg and a Buddhist monk. In June we brought Donna Hanelin, a top writing instructor, to give the group a three-hour workshop on a Saturday. This is only a partial list of workshops and classes we have attended in the past seven years.

So, as smart writer bees, we gather lots of nectar. And we turn it into honey and bring it back to our group, sharing our new skills with our other members. Everybody in our group benefits from cross pollination.

Chapter 9

If I'd Married
the Other One

Anne Da Vigo

THERE IS A LOT OF POWER for the writer in What If. In this section, we wrote for 20 minutes on the same What If from the past, "If I'd Married the Other One." The prompt led us to root around in some emotions that often have potential for good writing: regret, relief, anger, and reflection. The trouble caused by missed chances and bad choices never fails to spur our work, turning misfortune into useful nuggets of inspiration.

Using What If also is a good technique for moving beyond a stuck place or for tickling the imagination.

I am writing a novel about a women's professional basketball coach. My coach at one point is stymied by how to get better cooperation from her team captain. As the author, I had also run out of ideas. I sat down with a piece of paper and jotted ten What Ifs. What if the coach fired her player as team captain? What if she heaped her with undeserved praise? What if she bribed her? What if she invoked the goddess of the moon? My solution: the wily coach did some major female bonding—the two of them went shopping.

What Ifs allow you to shake off that feeling that your writing is wearing concrete overshoes. You can be weird or be silly, move to the center of the earth or the farthest galaxy, tap your fantasies or your dark side. In other words, be creative.

If I'd Married the Other One

Tom Fante

If we'd married the other one..." Agnes said. Agnes and I were sitting in her parlor drinking tea out of little cups ornamented with yellow flowers. I thought: who is this "we?" How like Agnes to address herself as "we" (the royal we), when she was, well, just a "she." I took a sip of green-colored tea. She was Agnes, plain old Agnes; she wasn't royalty; she was no Elizabeth Rex, no Helen of Troy to go around thinking people years later would be writing books about her. She was Agnes, violet sweater, little feather hat, 5' 3" with flabby white skin, liver-spotted, wearing thick socks and a feather boa. And as always, she had on red shoes.

Agnes wasn't a "we." No. She was barely an "I," if it came down to it, but she lived in a world of dreams. I set my cup down. "What do you mean by we?" I asked.

I remembered her husband, my Uncle Mitch, good old "Mitch the Itch," always scratching his grizzled chin and running bony fingers through his thin gray hair. The last time I had seen Mitch was five years ago. We were in church and he, dead in his coffin. He didn't look any deader than he ever had. I was just a kid then, and I pinched my leg through the pocket of my pants to keep from laughing. Mitch loved practical jokes; maybe this was another one, a trick on the rest of us. Maybe he wasn't dead. Aunt Agnes had sniffed, and a big orange tear had rolled down her powdered cheek pushing a small red ruff of rouge before it. It had rolled all the way to her chin, and there it lingered. The lavender candles guttered; they dimmed and sparked and tiny curls of black smoke rose up. Their smell filled the room and lay over the reek of the gardenias. The priest said "Amen," and bells jangled, the organ pealed and it was all over. We had all filed out, Agnes first. The memory of the funeral was still strong. I shook my head slightly to snap myself back to the present.

So who was this "other one" royal Agnes should have married? I thought again. Was he still alive? Was that it? Did he perhaps have a bit more tread left than Mitch had? Did he come with a better warranty?

"What did you mean Auntie?" I repeated.

With a long sigh, she eased herself onto her fat sofa, the awful one embroidered with fruits from grapes to bananas. From her ample bosom, she withdrew a stained cloth hankie. She pressed it to her nose, gave a honk, and

80 / coffee and ink

then let out a sob. She rolled the hankie around her bloated index finger like a cocoon shrouding a fat caterpillar.

"My life hasn't been an easy one, no, but I was young once, ooh! And such a beauty!" (I didn't believe it could be true.) "And I loved," she said. "Ah, to love; can you begin to understand?"

"I want to understand Auntie," I replied.

I was sure that whatever she had to say would amaze me me. It would be lie from beginning to end, of course, but a lie so stupendous that reality would shrink away from it, like a slug exposed to a pinch of salt. I set my tiny teacup on the table as I waited for her next words.

"Another time," she chirped.

☙

If I'd Married the Other One

Deb Marois

They sat in tense silence as Terry repeatedly turned the key in hopes that the old Ford pickup would catch and turn over. In the quiet, Carole inhaled the cold winter air that threatened to make her nostrils stick together. She turned her breath toward the passenger side window and watched as fog spread across the dirty pane. Her finger slowly traced the shape of a heart.

Suddenly, Terry pounded his fist on the dash so hard that Carole was certain the brittle plastic would crack under the pressure. "Son offa bitch!" The words ricocheted across the cramped cab and reverberated inside her head.

Carole carefully kept her face turned to the window so Terry wouldn't see the mixture of contempt, pity, and disgust in her eyes. The years had given her ample practice in hiding her true feelings behind a blank expression, but lately she was having trouble keeping the resentment from showing. She continued her drawing by piercing the heart with a long, thin arrow.

Terry glared in her direction before he jumped out and slammed the truck door with all the force he could muster. She watched the trail of his breath rise as he leaned under the hood and spewed obscenities.

Carole looked up at the night sky littered with stars, searching for the elusive one that only rarely streaks across the heavens. Her mind trailed back to high school and the one who got away. She had heard through the grapevine that Mark had graduated from college at the top of his class; he was probably now a successful computer whiz or accountant. She pictured him in a suit, still handsome with uncalloused hands and a gentle voice.

Bam, bam, bam! Carole jumped in her seat again as Terry hammered on her window. She groped for the handle and slowly cracked the window open. His words rushed in along with the cold air. "Give it a try now," he commanded before stomping off to watch the inner workings of the engine. Before sliding behind the wheel, with one full sweep of her outstretched hand, Carole smeared the dripping heart across the pane and willed herself to erase the longing for another life.

❦

If I'd Married the Other One

Virginia Kidd

*D*arren Landro was a salesman for Kimberly-Clarke, the Kleenex people. Still is. He gets all the Kleenex he wants for free. I guess. I mean, I never asked him, but surely he does, don't you think?" Carla's voice had an edge of self-consciousness, like a teenager talking about a cool football player. It was her turn to tell us about an early love.

No one answered her. Meredith poured more merlot in her glass, swirled it, and held it up to the light. Ruth reached for a cookie, then tucked her feet under her on the moss green sofa. Finally I spoke. "Did you think of marrying Darren?"

Carla answered, "Well, I mean—only just a thought, you know. Bill and I married when I was twenty, so I guess I didn't really."

Bill was a young attorney then and Carla was Miss Jackson County. We'd all known her. We'd all known each other for twenty years.

"But Darren was…" The fire crackled as a log fell in a shower of sparks. Carla stared at the dancing flames as though they held answers. "Darren was so—gentle." The word escaped like the last puff of air out of a half full balloon. No one had ever called Bill Wainwright gentle. Carla's eyes seemed sunk in hollows above skin Lancôme could not save. "Someone else—" she cried; "It's someone else's turn." She grabbed her wine.

"Meredith," I said, to move attention from Carla more than anything else. I wasn't the leader, but I was the unmarried one, used to fighting my own battles in the corporate world. Taking over was natural. "Tell us about the one you didn't marry."

"There was never anyone but Robbie," Meredith lied, so innocently that Carla shot wine out her nose and Ruth choked on her cookie. "Okay, if I'd married the other one—" Meredith paused. "Well, Carla, the other one was Bill. If I'd done that, I guess you'd have lots of Kleenex."

"And you would need them," Carla said. She stared into the fire, her eyes not moving from the flames.

It had started as such a simple game. How did it get so deadly so fast?

If I'd Married the Other One

Barbara Link

If I'd married Roger I'd be living in the house on stilts with the oak tree soaring through the redwood deck. Below, Dry Creek would trickle, trickle and flood every hundred years. Black lace shadows from the valley oaks would dapple the gray concrete floors and I'd worry about the rat-face possum coming in to crunch the cat food.

We'd fly in the Cessna 179 to Minden, Nevada for the weekend as I searched for air traffic and read aerial maps. We'd avoid the towers of cumulus clouds, red wine (no drinking while flying) and the hot valley air. Or we'd wing to Carmel and drive up the coast to the Laguna Seca road race. I'd spot Paul Newman leaning against his race car and cradling a can of Bud. My fingertips tingle as I realize he's my height and in bed it'd be a perfect fit.

With Roger my nights would spin into worry. I'd set the alarm for 1 a.m. so I could drive by his watering holes in my blue bathrobe, wearing no makeup, looking for his car.

Every day at lunch, I'd hear his wheezing accordion laugh—the long, long intake of breath until his face gleamed as red as a LA sunset. Then the bursting into the "Heh, heh, heh," causing everyone to laugh with relief that the Heimlich wouldn't be needed after all.

I'd hide my assets in a false credit union account, a sewing tin, and the inside pockets of my purple ski parka, so that when the relationship crashed into smoke and rain after years of bliss and misery, I'd have a grubstake to begin again.

∽

If I'd Married the Other One

Anne Da Vigo

It's May, and the snow has melted. Time to shed my wool socks and winter boots. I kneel on the bedroom rug and rummage through a pile of Tucker's cowboy boots, all of them muddy and smelling like wet leather. Finally, at the bottom of the pile I find my running shoes that were new last fall but now have a serious case of mildew.

Tucker comes in from the kitchen. "The Lookout Point Trail is open. Why don't I declare the office closed and we can hike there this afternoon?" he says.

His beard hasn't been trimmed for months and he looks like Jeremiah Johnson. The local barber locked up his shop and moved to the desert when the snow began to fall. Tucker never got around to trimming it himself. "I'm making Hell-and-Gone Chili. Do we have any dried Fresno chilies?" Tucker says.

"In the jar on the shelf marked chilies," I say. "How come you can snowshoe across the mountains in winter without getting lost but you can't find your way around the kitchen?"

"They weren't in my usual place," he says.

"You mean, where you left them in August, the last time you made chili?" I whack the toe of my running shoe against the floor and shake it. A scorpion falls out and makes a dash for freedom, but I flatten it. "I've found a place on the Internet where I can get banned insecticides. This year, the creepy crawlers are history."

"You've got to relax. Live and let live," Tucker says. "By the way, Big Bob got into the garbage shed last night. Tore the hinges off and spread trash everywhere."

"I told you we needed to put new doors on it. Did you clean up the mess?"

"Not yet."

"How long has it taken him to get back from the high country this time? A month? I wish I had a gun."

Tucker picks up my cat, Mighty Mo, off the bed, where she is nipping at the burrs and foxtails that cling to her fur. "Lucky you were inside my girl, or you might have been a midnight snack." Mighty Mo claws him viciously on the wrist. "Ow. Did I deserve that?" Tucker says.

"How many times have I told you, she doesn't like being disturbed while she's grooming?"

Tucker sucks his wrist bone. "I think we're out of onions and red wine for the chili. I need to make a grocery run."

"Wait a minute. I thought we were going to Lookout Point."

"We can still go. It's only an hour to Creighton's in Coarsegold."

"Two hours round trip, if you drive 70 in a 45 zone. You can't afford another ticket."

Tucker chuckles. "Don't worry. They won't throw the police chief in jail."

∞

If I'd Married The Other One

Shauna L. Smith

Which one? Gary. Of course, Gary, the boy who was eighteen along with me, innocent, unobtrusive, creative, solid. The young man who understood how relationships worked, listened deeply, negotiated automatically. Who didn't play into my neurotic games, couldn't understand my insanity. Gary whose mother became my surrogate mom for years after he correctly refused to have anything to do with me.

We met in the Catskill Mountains employment agency, where high schoolers and college kids waited to get weekend work in the borscht circuit hotel dining rooms to earn cash for college. We spent our time playing cards or chess, reading Sartre, standing around, talking, arguing, flirting, complaining. Every time the phone rang we'd race over to Big Al's cluttered desk and beg for the new job, whether we were qualified or not.

Gary and I became a couple, hanging around together, in the Catskills and back home in the city. He was a fine photographer and wanted to be an architect. He valued my poems.

One weekend afternoon Gary left his job at a nearby hotel and hitchhiked to my hotel for the couple of hours we had between lunch and dinner. I was resting on a bench when he arrived, and after a few words and a hug he lay his thin long form along the bench, dropped his head into my lap and fell sound asleep. I sat there seething and after a few minutes impatiently moved my legs so that his head jerked around. He awoke to me accusing him of selfishly ignoring me. "You don't care about me at all," I yelled, stricken with indignation. "Why did you even bother to come here?"

Gary's face is bruised from sleep, and he is incredulous as he stands, tall and lanky, before me. "What are you talking about?" he asks in his soft-spoken way. I turn to walk away, mortified. He follows me, takes my hand, looks in my eyes. "I was tired, that's all. You know I've been working for days straight. I felt safe with you, like I could finally let down and relax. I wasn't trying to hurt you."

I struggle through the crashing memories that are distorting his words into a scramble. My mother screams at my father. "You don't think of anyone but yourself, do you, Sam?"

"Miss High and Mighty," he hollers back, not missing a beat. "I bet you think you do?"

"Bullshit," I answer Gary, and walk off haughtily to my room, unable to disentangle the voices inside and outside of me.

It took another fifteen years to unravel them, and how I wish I could go back again, to feel the weight of Gary's head in my lap once more, and love and comfort him, and apologize for the many times I was unable to think of anyone but myself.

∽

Chapter 10

Expanding Your Writers Group

Shauna L. Smith

A FEW MONTHS AGO at a downtown poetry reading, one of the poets, a talented, elegantly-coifed woman named Barbara, invited me to check out her Monday night writers group, since mine had recently dissolved.

As the only therapist in our writers group—although doubtless not the only one who's been on the sorry end of the couch— I tend to be especially aware of group process. Observing myself as a new member, I notice that while seasoned members are searching for the right word to describe hair color or rocks, I am dwelling on how to fit into the established group. I sometimes find myself caught in a quagmire of what is appropriate to share, not only in the writing but also in the group meeting.

In a group that is just forming, each person participates in the vision as it is clarified and, in the process, personalities, needs, and relationships evolve. In an already-formed group, rules, styles, and relationships (specific and subtle) have already been established, and these can be difficult for a new member to unravel.

In our group, since we meet in an anonymous place and the focus is more on literary than on self-expository writing, self-revelation comes through only in remnants that have to be woven together. In my former writers group, carpooling to each other's homes gave us a chance to talk on a personal level as well as to know people through our lifestyles. (Our homes reportedly tell more about us than personality tests do.)

As writers often tend to be introverts rather than extroverts who can take a group by storm, it would be good to have some kind of introductory ritual so feelings and direction can be shared. Group members may have mixed feelings about new people coming in to their already-established "family." Hopefully your group has decided ahead of time whether and when and who you want to add to your group. Also, what to do in case problems arise, such as someone coming in with a vision that is inconsistent with the one your group wants to keep. To avoid headaches, choose wisely and be clear about how you want your group to work. Here are some ideas to make this transition more graceful:

• Have someone be the designated "outreach" person with whom the new member can communicate (not quite a sponsor, just a friend). You can rotate the responsibility.

• Take time out to seriously introduce yourselves within the first month This could even be done through a free write. Share at least a few basics, such as who is in your family, what your work is, and what moves and inspires you.

• Explain how changes are decided upon, if there is a method in place.

• Have a list of members, with addresses, phone numbers and e-mail addresses ready to give out.

• If there are rules or styles that have evolved over the years, a brief handout could help. If we had one, it might look like this:

Welcome to our Writers Group!
We meet Mondays around 6:30 p.m. at Bella Bru coffee shop for a couple of hours.
We have a box of prompts, which you are welcome to add to.
We generally write from two prompts a night, for about twenty minutes each.
In spite of the noise, we valiantly share our stories.
Feedback is about what is memorable, but wow is acceptable.
Sometimes some of us buy dinner, sometimes not; it's very random.
You don't need to let anyone know whether or not you'll be there (perhaps based on Natalie Goldberg's idea of asking a friend to meet for a free write at a coffee shop, blocking off "writing time" regardless of whether or not your friend shows up).

All this shouldn't take a long time and could make the inclusion process easier for everyone, minimize misunderstandings, and help you keep new members if you want them to stay.

Chapter 11

Juicy Prompts and Creative Jump Starts

Deb Marois

FROM OBSERVING THE REAL-LIFE characters in your local greasy spoon to attending a women's basketball game to better understand movement, teamwork and competition, the writer sees a world full of rich sources for writing. Every writer—and writers group—needs a jump start, and the easiest place to begin is with the world around you. Seeing the seemingly mundane with new eyes and describing its rich detail can transform a simple, everyday occurrence or object into material for your next novel, essay, or poem. Here are some ticklers that may get your creative thoughts squirming:

- Photographs or magazine pictures
- Objects on your dresser or table top
- The view from your office window
- Obituaries
- Personal ads
- Conversation overheard in the grocery store or coffee shop
- Scents—cotton dipped in wine, cinnamon
- Things that stimulate your sense of touch: Snakeskin
- First sentence from favorite books
- Something you see every day
- Cemetery headstones
- Letters cut up into short phrases—Christmas newsletters work well
- Fortune cookie predictions
- Postcards
- Newspaper or tabloid headlines
- Quotes from daily calendars

Here are some of the Monday Night Writers Group's favorite prompts:
- Elvis would be 67 today.
- Simile exercise—
    - as cold as
    - as lonely as

- The naming of pets
- You can redo one act from your past. What do you do? What changes as a result?
- Look around your home and pick out items that have particular meaning. Write the history of one of them.
- Why can't you throw that old thing away?
- Create a crowd scene—voice in an airport, restaurant, locker room, etc.
- Martha straightened up for a moment and arched her back, then rested on the hoe.
- Getting to elementary school
- Trapped on a bus in a snow storm or in a cab with a Hell's Angel in a traffic jam
- Where you were when…
- If I'd married the other one
- A childhood vacation
- Almost death
- A brief encounter
- A good Christmas
- My childhood room
- People I went to elementary school with
- Anne's house always made him hungry
- Viewpoint of a child
- Discovering skeletons
- Describe feelings very skillfully
- Embarrassing moment
- Romantic moment
- Angry moment
- New gangs
- Car deal
- Part-time job
- I don't remember
- The back burner
- A traumatic/dramatic environmental event
- One-sentence description of a person
- If bricks could talk
- Choose a body part and write praise to it; don't give in to humor.
- However, she has huge feet
- Since I don't like to sleep on the ground…
- What secrets does your pet keep from you?
- Things keep changing and yet they stay the same
- Sabotage in the workplace
- Small things people do if they don't respect authority
- A behavior that irritates you and what it says about you
- A hideout

- Behind lace curtains
- An early memory
- Tabloid story
- What's under your house?
- We ate Chinese
- A high school senior is about to flunk out
- Things I do after midnight
- What do news anchors, weathercasters, and sports anchors talk about five minutes before they go on air?
- My favorite relative
- A tattoo
- If I let myself admit it
- Small regrets
- What goes without saying?
- A description in the style of Raymond Chandler
- If you had to pose nude
- The last straw and how you arrived at this point
- A closed space
- In a state of disarray
- Use these words: kneel, heat, wooden door; write as many paragraphs as you can using all three.
- Your character collects hats
- He slumped down in his chair and everything about the way he looked could be summed up in one word.
- Don't make me hurt you
- We need to have courage to jump into this mess
- Show how a good deed can backfire
- So, enough of that
- Her father began by saying, "It's time to tell you something."
- In the lines of her face, I saw…
- There was something I always wanted from you
- Gossip
- The right size for a bachelor
- The quiet ones
- Dangerous ride
- The red wagon
- Taking a detour
- Your inauguration speech when you are sworn in as president
- When all is said and done
- Clichés
- Writing contest rules (e.g., 50-word short story)

About Writing: Web Sites and Books

There are numerous sources of wisdom from many other talented writers. For those of you who love to soak up ideas from other authors, here are some sources to get you started.

Web Sites
The Art of Writing Instant Muse Utilities
http://www.webcom.com/wordings/artofwrite/inspiration.html

Creative Writing Prompts
http://www.creativewritingprompts.com/

Personal Journaling Magazine
http://www.journalingmagazine.com/

Suspense Writing Prompts
http://www.eduplace.com/rdg/hmll/purple/dark/prompts.html

Writing Prompts or Story Starters
http://www.angelfire.com/ks/teachme/prompts.html

Books
Berg, Elizabeth. *Escaping into the Open: The Art of Writing True*. New York: HarperCollins, 1999.

Browne, Renni and Dave King. *Self-Editing for Fiction Writers: How to Edit Yourself into Print*. New York: Harper Collins, 1993.

Cameron, Julia. *The Artist's Way*. New York: Jeremy P. Tarcher-Putnam, 1992.

__. *The Right to Write: An Invitation and Initiation into the Writing Life*. J.P. Tarcher, 1999.

Frey, James. *How to Write a Damn Good Novel*. New York: St. Martin's Press, 1987.

—. *How to Write a Damn Good Novel II*. New York: St. Martin's Press, 1994.

Gardner, John. *The Art of Fiction*. 1983. New York: Vintage-Random House, 1991.